MW01065184

Numbers 6:24-26

Best wishes and
God bless you
Margaret Weston

HOW DO I KNOW I KNOW GOD?

All profit made by the author from this book is donated to Tearfund.

Tearfund is a Christian international aid and development agency working globally to end poverty and injustice, and to restore dignity and hope in some of the world's poorest communities.

Tearfund operates in more than fifty countries around the world. As well as being present in disaster situations and recovery through their response teams, they speak out on behalf of poor people on the national and international stage by petitioning governments, campaigning for justice and raising the profile of key poverty issues wherever they can.

Find out more at www.tearfund.org

Copyright: 2011 Margaret Weston

ISBN-13: 978-1477561065
ISBN-10: 1477561064

First printed 2012 – Reprinted May 2013

Unless stated otherwise, all Scripture quotations in this publication are from the HOLY BIBLE, NEW INTERNATIONAL VERSION ® NIV ® Copyright © 1973, 1978, 1984, 2011 by Biblica, Inc.®. All rights reserved worldwide.

The "NIV" and "New International Version" are trademarks registered in the United States Patent and Trademark Office by Biblica, Inc.®. Use of either trademark requires the permission of Biblica, Inc.®.

This is the first book in the
'How do I know?' series

There are three books in this series:
How do I know I know God?
How do I know what God wants me to do?
How do I know God answers prayer?

HOW DO I KNOW I KNOW GOD?

CONTENTS

INTRODUCTION
WHAT IF IT'S TRUE AFTER ALL?

I have often been asked the question, 'How do you know you know God?' Sometimes the same question is phrased differently – 'how do you know it's not just your imagination?' or 'you may think God hears you but how do you really know?' Sometimes people are polite, sometimes they are not, but it always come down to this basic question – how do you really know? The answer is, I suppose, very simple but also very profound. I know I know God because I have a relationship with him. Relationships make things very real – there are highs and lows, good times and bad times in real relationships and so it is with my relationship with God. But if I say I have a relationship with God we must first of all believe that it is possible to have such a relationship otherwise all that I say must be untrue. I have therefore divided this book into two parts. In the first part I seek to show that it is indeed possible to have a relationship with God and in the second part I try to explain something of the nature of my own relationship with God.

Before we begin though let me first ask you a question. Have you ever considered this - suppose it really is true after all?

Even when we are Christians we can still sometimes doubt this so whatever your current beliefs I am asking you to suppose for a moment that it is actually true. What if God created the earth (and you and me) because he wanted to have a relationship with *you*? What if he wanted company and companionship as many of us do? What if he decided on a vast plan so that he could have the company of you and me – and many like us – for time and for eternity? What if he wanted to show his love for something – or someone – or many people – or indeed you personally and decided on a plan in order to do so?

What if you were created specifically so that you could have a relationship with God? What if he gave the very best he could – his only Son – in order to demonstrate his mighty love for you? What if his Son Jesus came to this earth – specifically for *you* – so that he could show *you* what God was like? After showing you what God was like, what if Jesus then died a horrific death on a cross so that he could show you, beyond any question, how much God loves *you*?

11

What if Jesus was so perfect that death could not hold him in its power so he rose again? What if he is now in heaven at the right hand of God waiting for you to reach out to him and longing that you might really come to know God by having a relationship with him? What if he looks down now and day after day he is waiting patiently for you to come to him and say 'thank you for all you have done for me and I would love to know who you are and have a relationship with you'?

What if, at the end of your life, you find you have missed out on the best and the greatest experience – to know God through Jesus Christ - and then find out that you have missed the opportunity of spending eternity with him?

I ask you to consider this question as if you have never heard it before - what if it is all actually true after all? All those things you have heard about and either rejected or never really thought about – *What if these things are actually true?*

PART ONE

IS IT POSSIBLE TO KNOW GOD?

Chapter 1
IN THE BEGINNING

"In the beginning God created the heavens and the earth."

"Well, I don't believe in God"

"Do you think that has any effect?"

"What do you mean, does it have any effect – effect on what?"

"Effect on whether it is actually true of course."

"Oh I see. I suppose it doesn't much."

"Doesn't much? Actually it has no effect whatever on whether it is true or not. What you believe has no bearing on whether something is true or not. Just because you don't believe in God doesn't mean he doesn't exist. Either he does or he doesn't – irrespective of what you or I believe."

"Well yes, I suppose that must be true."

"And if he does exist and yet you don't believe in him – don't you think that could be rather a big mistake?"

"I hadn't really thought about it."

"Have you ever really looked into the question of whether it is true?"

"I've been to church and found it incredibly boring."

"That could be the fault of the church – or it could possibly (or probably!) be your fault. It doesn't make any difference as to whether God exists or not."

"No, I suppose it doesn't. So you believe in God then?"

"Yes, of course I do."

"But you can't prove he exists can you?"

"Well, that depends on what you mean by proof."

"You can't know for sure he exists."

"Yes I can – because I know him and have a relationship with him."

"That's easy enough to say but how do I know it's true?"

"Well, who do you think created the world then – or indeed, the universe?"

"I don't have a clue! I think maybe there was a big bang and there it was, or maybe it just happened somehow?"

"Wow – and you think I am the one who is deluded!"

"What do you mean?"

"How could something so wonderful 'just happen'? It takes more faith to believe that than it does to believe in God! Just look at the way God constantly reveals himself in creation. He paints wonderful sunsets and sunrises, creates stormy seas and majestic mountains. You look at a beautiful picture of a sunset and you admire the artist – but who do you think gave the artist the subject in the first place and then the talent to paint it?"

"I would have to think about that."

"Why do you have to make it so complicated? 'In the beginning God created the heavens and the earth' – that's plain enough isn't it?"

"Perhaps that is too simple!"

"Ah, I see. You would prefer an answer that needs a bit of your intellect and brain power, perhaps a solution that makes something of you – so you can show how intelligent you are in working it all out!"

"That's a bit unfair to say that just because I don't believe the same as you do. It's not that simple to me."

"I'm sorry if you think that's unfair but I don't suppose it was that simple to make the universe and maybe that's the problem for many of us."

"Yes, when I do think about it, I think that nature and the world around us is just so wonderful."

"So only someone very great could possibly have thought it all up in the first place and it must have been such a complicated task to put it all in place. That's the problem you see. If God tried to explain it and go through all the details of how he did it there is no way a human mind could understand it anyway. So, I expect he thought the best thing to say was just that he did it, rather than try to explain further."

"That does actually make sense to me. It would be a bit like trying to teach a three-year old about nuclear physics or something wouldn't it!"

"Actually, I think it would be a lot worse than that!"

Have you ever looked up at the beauty of the sky with a few wispy clouds against the brilliant blue? Have you ever looked up at the sky with a storm approaching, with the beauty and majesty of the inky black clouds as they speed towards you? Have you ever looked up at the clear night sky and seen the wonderful spectacle of the stars and realized there are just too many for you to number? Have you ever looked out to sea and marvelled at the colours as the skyline collides with the blue sky horizon? Have you ever seen it all change in an instant as the sea is stirred up with the wind and rain and suddenly a completely different picture emerges even as you watch?

Have you ever gazed at the mountains and wondered how they can be so huge and so majestic? Have you ever walked in the countryside and been amazed at just how many shades of green there can be and how beautiful it all is? Have you ever wondered how this all just 'happened'?

The Grand Design

If I show you a beautiful picture you would never say it just 'happened'. You would know there had to be an artist and a design. If I show you an intricate engine you would know there had to be an engineer. If I show you a fabulous house you would know there had to be a builder. Why then, when I show you creation do you choose to believe it occurred as if by accident?

For me it is far more ridiculous to believe these things happened 'by accident' than it is to believe that there is and was a grand design and a great Creator. Far more difficult to believe that everything is held in place by chance than to believe that the Creator created laws in the universe in order to ensure everything operates as it does. To ensure the sun is just far enough away to give light but not to burn earth to a cinder. To ensure night follows day and winter follows summer and nature follows a certain course.

However, if I choose not to believe in God then I must have an alternative – however ridiculous that alternative, it is better than believing in God - so I think. Because if I believe in God then there will be consequences from so doing and I may even have to change the way I live. So I prefer to call it all an accident, or a big bang theory, or nature, in order to avoid acknowledging God or perhaps just not to think about it at all.

An Email from a Friend

I received an email from you, my friend, the other day. It was a forwarded copy of an email – you know, the kind that get passed around the internet – and it showed the most fabulous pictures of animals, mountains, the sea, the sky and so on. It had a message at the beginning which said; 'Nature at its best - I don't know what is more fantastic, the pictures or the photographer'. It made me sad because I thought, 'but what about the One who created both the photographer and the subjects of the pictures?'

Why are we happy to praise the creation and the one who takes the photographs but we do not want to acknowledge the Creator?

How do you think God feels when all he has created is just taken for granted and when all he has done, for your enjoyment, is simply put down to 'nature' or some other nebulous identity.

I ask you again, when you look at a beautiful painting do you really think it has just somehow created itself? When you look at an engine or piece of machinery do you really think that somehow it just 'appeared'? When you look at a dress or a house do you really think that somehow it just designed itself? Why then when you look at nature do you suppose that there is no designer, no grand plan and no God?

The first few words of the Bible are, 'In the beginning'. What better place to start than at the beginning! And yet what controversy surrounds this simple statement. When was the beginning? How long ago was the beginning? How can there even have been a beginning? When did God begin? - and numerous other pointless questions and controversies. Why is it that man, especially intellectual man, cannot accept that simple statement? God has said that, 'In the beginning, God created the heavens and the earth' – he hasn't told us how long ago that was and he never intended to do so. I wonder if God smiles as he looks down at the pride of man that thinks that by his intelligence and his intellect he can ever come anywhere near to understanding what God has done. Why is it so difficult to simply accept the explanation that, 'In the beginning God created'?

Why Not Believe?

There are many reasons of course why we choose not to believe in God creating the world but I want to highlight only two. Firstly, that it is too easy and man in his pride wants it be very difficult so that he can prove how wonderful he is in working it out – which of course he never will. Secondly, we have to believe that God exists in order to believe that he created, and that requires faith. How often our pride gets in the way and never more so than when dealing with the things relating directly to God. We have to put pride aside and accept that our tiny brain is not able to understand all the hows and the whys and we have to ask God for faith, if we are to rightly understand anything at all.

19

Are you too proud to ask God for faith? Don't you want the opportunity of knowing the Creator of the universe? Don't you want to know the One who says, 'In the beginning' and knows exactly when that was, even if he does not wish to reveal that knowledge to you at this moment in time?

As a parent cannot explain everything to a child because of the child's limited understanding, so God cannot explain many things to us because our intellect is too small to grasp it. So, with a child's trust and a child's faith we have to put away our pride and come to God and ask for faith. What peace we can have as we put aside senseless questions - knowing that even if we were told the answer we wouldn't understand - and simply have faith in God.

Knowing the Creator

So let's suppose that this first part of our story is true after all. You might well then be thinking that, if it is true, then it means that God is majestic and mighty and far beyond our human comprehension. It means he is too great to try to encompass or describe with mere human words. Some people do get to this point of belief but no further. There are many religions that will point you to a 'god' or even some 'gods' and many people will try to worship such gods in a way that they believe pleases such a god. However, I do not know of any that can offer you a way to know God personally for yourself and to have a personal relationship with him. This excludes of course Christianity, if we call that a 'religion'. The difficulty with Christianity is that if it is merely a 'religion' to me then I, also, will never have the joy of knowing God for myself. If Christianity is merely a 'religion' for me then, in that sense, it is no different to any other religion. This book however is not about my 'religion' it is about how I know that I know God.

In many ways I can understand those who believe in God and then leave it there. The Bible says, "You believe that there is one God. Good! Even the demons believe that – and shudder." (James 2:19) - as if to say, that it must be utter madness not even to believe that there is a God! But how sad if we only believe in God without having a glimpse into his plans and purposes for us and without ever coming to know him personally.

Maybe though, you do believe in God but you might be thinking that if creation is all according to his design and plan and purpose then where does that leave you (and me)? Surely that would make it impossible for me to have a relationship with such a One. If God is so great and far beyond my comprehension, such that he could not begin to explain creation to me because I would not understand the explanation, then how could I even begin to know him, let alone have a relationship with him?   He is so awesome and I am so small and insignificant when compared with such majesty and might – how could I possibly ever know God?

I hope you might be thinking that because if you are, you are in good company! One of the Psalms says 'what is mankind that you are mindful of them, human beings that you care for them? (Psalm 8:4)' as if to say, why would such a majestic God bother about small insignificant man. That is a very good question and so we will explore this further in the next chapter.

O Lord My God

O Lord my God when I in awesome wonder
Consider all the works Thy hand hath made
I see the stars I hear the mighty thunder
Thy power throughout the universe displayed.

Then sings my soul my Saviour God to Thee
How great Thou art! How great Thou art!
Then sings my soul, my Saviour God to Thee
How great Thou art, how great Thou art!

When through the woods and forest glades I wander
And hear the birds sing sweetly in the trees
When I look down from lofty mountain grandeur
And hear the brook and feel the gentle breeze;

(Russian hymn)

Chapter 2
THE WORD BECAME FLESH

"I think I do want to know God, if that is possible, but I am merely human. My intellect is limited, my mind is so small. If I believe he made the heavens and the earth, then that is far beyond my comprehension. How can it be possible to know him? He is too great and I am too small."

"What if I tell you that he loves you and he wants to have a relationship with you."

"Well, that just makes me afraid. Long ago Moses asked to see the glory of God and God said that no one could see his face and live – (see Exodus 33:18-22). Where does that leave me?"

"Yes I see the problem and believe it or not God knew about this problem long before it occurred and was prepared to do something about it."

"Really? What has he done then?"

"Let me ask you a question. How do you feel about a baby? Are you afraid of a baby?'

"Oh no, I love babies. No one should be afraid of a baby."

"And he did not want you to be afraid of him, so he came down to earth as a baby.'

"Wow, that doesn't make much sense. Why would anyone want to do that?"

"Because God loves you and wants to have a relationship with you."

"But if he lives in such a fantastic place as heaven, why come to earth and live here with all the problems and sorrow that are here?"

"Because he loves you and wants to have a relationship with you. God wants you to know that he understands you completely. When you have problems and sorrow, he understands – because he has been through it all too. You are not talking to someone who doesn't understand – he has done this to show you that he does. You might not understand God, but he understands you!"

"Why would he do such a thing?"

"Because he loves you and wants to have a relationship with you."

"I still find that hard to believe. It doesn't make much sense to me."

"Much of what he does doesn't make sense to the natural mind. That's why the Bible tells you that the foolishness of God is greater than your wisdom – (see 1 Corinthians 1:25). Why else would he do such a thing if it were not for love?"

"I have heard people talk about God so loving the world that he gave his Son so this must be part of that story. You must be talking about when Jesus came to earth as a baby – what people call the Christmas story?"

"Yes that's right. Jesus came to earth in order to show you what God is like. Jesus said, "Anyone who has seen me has seen the Father" (John 14:9). So when you see what Jesus is like, you see God. When you see how he behaves, you see God. When you see his love for you, you see God's love. All that you can learn about Jesus tells you about God, because Jesus is God himself come down to earth in human form. Jesus is completely man (the only perfect man who was ever on earth) and completely God. You may have heard the name 'Immanuel' given to Jesus. That means 'God with us."

"God with us? So you are saying that because God wanted to have a relationship with us he came down to earth to be with us?"

"Yes that's right and it is what the Bible means when it says that 'the word became flesh and made his dwelling among us' (John 1:14), it is talking about Jesus!"

"Oh dear this is very difficult to comprehend. Perhaps your next chapter will have to be about Jesus, to try and explain how he has made it possible for us to have a relationship with God."

I could not write a book about knowing God without reference first and foremost to Jesus. It is through the person and the work of Jesus that we are able to know God. Without him it would be impossible. God is so great, so holy and so far above us, that he had to find a way to draw near to us in order that we could have a relationship with him. Jesus says, 'I am the way and the truth and the life. No one comes to the Father except through me' (John 14:6).

God With Us

It has been said that history either points forward to Christ (BC) or it points backwards to him (AD). If you study the Bible you will find that it is centred on Jesus. The Old Testament points forward to his coming and the New Testament speaks about when he actually came to earth and what happened as a result of that. It speaks about his life here and about the New Covenant made with humankind as a result of his coming. We cannot have a relationship with God without the Lord Jesus Christ. God has arranged it so and we cannot have it any other way.

The name Jesus means 'Saviour' and the name 'Immanuel' (which we often only hear mentioned at Christmas time) means 'God with us'. The Bible tells us this name for Jesus in both the Old and New Testaments – Isaiah 7.14 'The virgin will conceive and give birth to a son, and will call him Immanuel.' Matthew 1.23 'The virgin will conceive and will give birth to a son, and they will call him Immanuel'.

Jesus – the Saviour who is able to 'save' us. Save us from what? Save us from *everything* that separates us from God and prevents us from having a relationship with him.

Immanuel – God with us. Think about that for a moment – *God with us*. Not just a representative of God but God himself, with us. God become man, God come to earth in human form in order to associate with us, show us that he knows what it is to be human and show us that he wants to have a relationship with us. If I, as a human, wanted to get close to a sparrow, so that I could show that I fully understood it and to make it possible for it to have a relationship with me, then I would have to become a sparrow. God, in his desire to have a relationship with us, became a man – completely human and yet also completely God – and lived on earth in order to demonstrate his love for me and show me how much he wants to have a relationship with me. Long ago King Solomon asked, "But will God really dwell on earth with humans?' – (2 Chronicles 6:18). Here at last was the answer – Immanuel, God with us.

In the Bible Jesus is also called 'the word' – 'The word became flesh and made his dwelling among us' (John 1:14). The original word in the Greek language is 'logos'. It is difficult to find an accurate English translation for this because of the scope of the word. Suffice to say here that it incorporates the idea of human reason together with divine or universal intelligence. Simply put, it shows God's desire to 'speak' with us and thus to form a relationship with us. The 'word became flesh' shows us God's desire and ability to link the human with the divine and provide the bridge which is necessary between the two if we are to ever be able to have a relationship with him.

God Provides The Way

So God has provided the way in which I can begin to know him. I can look at Jesus and see God. I can see the way Jesus behaves and know that is the way God acts. I can see his love, his compassion, his mercy, his humility and so much more and know that this is the love and the compassion and the mercy and the humility of God.

Humility – that is a word that is not used very much these days! It is particularly rarely used of those who seem to be very powerful or very important in man's eyes. Yet God was prepared to humble himself and come to earth. In Philippians, which is a book of the Bible in the New Testament, it tells us that, 'He humbled himself' (Philippians 2:8). To whom does this refer? It refers to Jesus himself. The One who is, in himself God, the Creator of the universe, humbled himself. Can you grasp just what that word 'humbled' really means in this particular instance? We read it so quickly but – the Creator of the universe, he who holds the stars in his hand, he who is greater than anything or anyone we can ever imagine, actually became man. The enormity of this should not pass us by and is perhaps why some find it so difficult to believe. It is so different from the pride and arrogance of humankind.

I understand that if we imagine the earth as the size of a golf ball and then tried to put it on the same giant screen as some of the bigger stars now discovered, then earth would not even register. Look up such names as Vy Canis Majoris or Antares on the internet and see how small earth is by comparison. Earth would not even register on the same page, let alone the tiny speck which would represent you and me. No wonder the Psalmist says, 'what is mankind that you are mindful of them,' (Psalm 8:4). And yet, God *humbled* himself. The Lord Jesus, who is God, *humbled* himself and came here as a man. No wonder we need faith to believe this because it is so unlike us! Why would he do such a thing? Suppose this is true, then why, why, why would he do such a thing?

It was because of his love for you and because he wanted – and still wants – to have a relationship with you!

So now I can know what God is like because Jesus came to earth to show me. Of course, there is a big difference between knowing *about* someone and actually *knowing* them through having a relationship with them. You may rightly think now that even if I accept that I can know about God because Jesus came, that still gives me no way of knowing him personally and having a relationship with him. I might see him as a wonderful person but still have no way of entering into a relationship with him. In fact, you might think, the more wonderful I find him to be, the less likely it will be that I can have a relationship with him as I am certainly not wonderful. Simply put, he is perfect and I am not! You may be thinking, I have lost count of all the things I am, and have done, which must make it impossible for me to have a relationship with a holy and perfect God. I hope you are thinking this and that, if you are, you will read on.

Meekness and Majesty[1]

Meekness and majesty
Manhood and Deity
In perfect harmony
The Man who is God
Lord of eternity
Dwells in humanity
Kneels in humility
And washes our feet.

Oh what a mystery
Meekness and majesty
Bow down and worship
For this is your God
This is your God.

(Graham Kendrick)

Chapter 3
SUCH LOVE

"Right, so perhaps I accept that God is the Creator and that Jesus came to earth in human form to show me what God is like. But if I believe the history books, Jesus also died on a cross. What was the point of all that?"

"It was all because of love. He wanted to show you just how much he loves you. He took the punishment for all the things you have ever done wrong so that you would be able to have a relationship with God. So that, in God's eyes, you could be perfect and without any sin put to your account."

"That's an old fashioned word isn't it, sin. I have heard Christians talk about 'sin' and they have said that I am a sinner – what does that mean exactly?"

"Have you ever done anything wrong?"

"Ah well yes I'm sure I have – I wouldn't claim to be perfect - after all, no one is, are they?"

"No that is quite right, no one (except Jesus) is perfect – the Bible says that too."

"Does it? I didn't know that."

"Yes it says that there is not one righteous – not even one (Romans 3:10). So when God looks down on earth there is not one person who can stand before him and tell him, honestly, that they are not a sinner."

"That must make him very sad."

"Yes it does but he is also very happy because when he looks on earth he does see many millions of people who are righteous in his eyes – even though they have sinned."

"How on earth (excuse the pun) can that be?"

"Well, would you agree that sin should be punished?"

"Oh yes certainly it should. It makes me mad when people get away with doing nasty things and they are not punished for it."

"So should *you* be punished for the nasty things you have said, or thought?"

"Oh dear, when you put it like that, I suppose I should. So have all these people that God sees as 'righteous' been punished for what they have done – you know, the score been settled sort of thing?"

"There has been punishment and the score has been settled but someone has taken all the punishment for them."

"Who would want to do something like that? It must be someone who loves them very much. I certainly wouldn't want to be punished for something I didn't do."

"Yes you are right about love. Jesus took all the punishment for sin when he died on the cross and shed his precious blood - yes you are right it was only because of love."

"Wow! That is hard to take in. So were all my sins covered then too?"

"Yes but only if that's what you want. You need to repent and accept what Jesus has done on your behalf (Acts 2:38)."

"Repent? That's another old fashioned word and I'm not sure I really understand what that means either!"

"It means being sorry or contrite about what you have done – or not done. It means that you agree with God that you are a sinner and that you need a Saviour. You realize that you are wrong and God is right."

"You mean just say sorry and then get on with my life?"

"No I don't mean that at all! The real meaning of repentance is a change of mind. You are sorry about your sin but you feel so bad about it that you want to change. It is a change of mind from your own way and your own thoughts to God's way. You want him to control your life and you want to do what pleases him rather than to please yourself."

"But if I repent and accept what Jesus has done for me it seems to be cheating somehow – too easy."

"It wasn't easy for Jesus. Part of what repentance means is that you realize, to some extent, just what a terrible price was paid for your sin. The Lord Jesus gave up everything for me (and you) and he shed his blood on the cross for me (and for you)."

"I think I understand that but what if I don't repent and don't want to accept what Jesus has done?"

"Well that is your choice. You will then need to explain all you have done to God and accept the punishment for your sins yourself after death. True judgement comes after death and that is when you will have to meet with God and accept the consequences of your decision."

"I think I understand now. Either I can accept what Jesus has done and know that all my sins have been taken away as far as God is concerned, or I can decide to take the punishment myself after death."

"Yes that's right. I have accepted what Jesus has done and have a relationship with him now which will last through time and then into eternity. What choice will you make?"

Many people know that Christians believe that Jesus came to earth as a baby, died on the cross, was buried in a tomb, rose again on the third day and ascended into heaven. We hear about it during an occasional visit to a church around Christmas time or Easter time, or we see it referred to on a Christmas or Easter card or on a placard outside a church. Have *you* ever thought about it though for more than a few passing moments? Have you ever considered whether it is true and if it is what it might mean for you personally? What if it is all true? What if the reason it happened was so that God could show *you* how much he loves *you*? Would you really reject such a love?

God's Love

The Bible tells me, and I believe it, that when man was first on the earth he was in a relationship with God. How close that relationship was I do not know but I wonder how much man really knew about the love of God – how could he do so unless he had some way of knowing it? Life was just wonderful and I expect he took it all for granted, never knowing anything else. Can we know love without knowing hate? Can we know good without knowing evil? These are big questions and I ask them only for you to think about, I do not presume to know the answers. Then, of course, sin entered the world through man's disobedience to God and the relationship that there was between God and man, was broken. Did this take God by surprise? Of course not! He knew he had the answer to this and a way to show man just how much he loved him.

So, as we know, Adam chose to disobey God and sin entered the world through disobedience. We know that the 'wages of sin is death' (Romans 6:23) and that is why each of us must die. Adam was the 'first man' – imperfect and earthly and he represented the first order or type of man that God created. However, Jesus was the 'second Adam' – perfect and heavenly and he is the first and the best representation of the second order or type of man that God has created. Just as we are by birth like Adam, so we can by 'new birth' become like Jesus and eventually join him in heaven. (To understand 'new birth' you will need to read later in this book about the Holy Spirit.) So, the Bible tells us that sin (and therefore death) entered the world through Adam and broke our relationship with God, but Jesus came in order to restore that relationship and, in so doing, show us just how much we are loved by God.

'For since death came through a man, the resurrection of the dead comes also through a man. For as in Adam all die, so in Christ all will be made alive.' You can find this in the Bible in 1 Corinthians 15:21-22 and read more about God's plans for us there.

We have already seen that Jesus came into the world to show us what God is like. He was the only perfect man and therefore the only man who was qualified to take on himself the punishment for sin. There was no reason for Jesus to die because he had no sin of his own and thus the 'wages of sin is death' did not apply to him. He could therefore take on the sins of the world. His sacrifice was a perfect sacrifice, for God demands no less. There was a great man who lived in the eleventh century called Anselm of Canterbury. I love his explanation of the death of Jesus when he says,

"No member of the human race except Christ ever gave to God, by dying, anything which that person was not at some time going to lose as a matter of necessity. Nor did anyone ever pay a debt to God which he did not owe. But Christ, of his own accord, gave to his Father what he was never going to lose as a matter of necessity and he paid on behalf of sinners, a debt which he did not owe."[2]

I expect you hear people talk about God being a God of love - which is true - but we sometimes forget that he is also a God of justice and righteousness. If sin were to go unpunished then God would not be righteous. He had to ensure that his wrath against sin was satisfied and it must be perfectly satisfied. So Jesus died on the cross and bore the penalty for your sins and for my sins and for the sins of the whole world. In that death sin was defeated and the requirements of a just and righteous God were met, once and for all. At the same time God demonstrated his extraordinary love for humanity – that includes me and it includes you. The reason Jesus died was not for his own sin but for your sins and mine. I am (and you are) now left with a choice – I can either accept what has been done on my behalf and say "thank you" or I can say "no thank you, I prefer to do it my way and I will accept the punishment for my sins myself".

So it had to be Jesus that died as he is the only perfect man – the first man of the new order that God has planned. To quote Anselm again, when speaking of the recompense necessary for sin, he says, 'no-one can pay except God and no-one ought to pay except man: it is necessary that a God-Man should pay it.'[3]

The cross of Christ

Jesus did not just die, he died on a cross. It was one of the cruellest means of execution available at that time. It was so cruel that it was abolished in AD315 because it was considered too inhumane. So Jesus did not just die, he suffered the awful agony of dying on a cross. In addition to this, his precious blood was shed. You may know that when the soldier pierced the side of Jesus to make sure he was dead, both blood and water flowed out. I understand that blood and water is a sign that someone is actually dead but there is a greater significance for us. Did you know that a covenant sealed with blood commits both parties to each other for ever? All they have belongs to the other person. So, the fact that Jesus shed his precious blood for me means that God has made a commitment to me for ever! If I accept what God has provided, then he will never renege on his promise of salvation and eternal life! Isn't that a wonderful thought? It certainly is for me.

The water is also significant as a symbol of cleansing. I am washed clean from my sins because I have accepted that Jesus died *for me*. Such love is just too great for me to comprehend but I can thank him for it nonetheless.

My way or God's way?

Can you think of a greater love than this? That someone should choose to give his life for you? When there was no reason that he should die – he was the only man who never did anything wrong – he still chose to die for you. Not only did he die for you but he accepted the full punishment for all the wrong things you have said and done. He took on himself the sins of the whole world so that anyone who is prepared to accept what he has done on their behalf can be saved. What amazing love!

You may not think you have done much wrong. You may compare yourself with a murderer or a thief and think you are pretty good. I have to tell you that you are using the wrong comparison! You have to compare yourself against the man who met God's standards – the perfect man – and now where do you stand? It is God who is the Creator and Judge and it is God that sets the standards not you. You might think you are better than your neighbour (although only God knows whether that is true) but even if you are, would you still like to justify all you have done (or not done) and all you have thought against a standard of perfection?

We often hear that a favourite song is "I did it my way", not realising that far from being a compliment for ourselves or someone else, it is actually the problem with many of our lives. We choose to do it our own way – not God's way – and we suffer the consequences of this. In our conversation above we spoke about repentance. Repentance towards God means we no longer want to do it our way but God's way. Repentance means having a true and deep remorse for all we have been and all we are. It means a change of mind so that we turn away from sin and towards God, acknowledging that he is right and we are wrong. It is God alone who is able to grant us repentance (2 Timothy 2:25).

Each of us has a choice. God has made us and given us freewill. We can make decisions for ourselves but each decision has a consequence. We can accept the provision that God has made for us to have a relationship with him or we can reject it. The consequence of accepting is that we will be able to enter into a long (indeed eternal) relationship with God which begins while we are here on earth and then continues when we are with him after death and enjoying eternal life.

The consequence of rejecting the offer is very serious. Not only does it mean that we reject the opportunity of entering into a relationship with God while here on earth but it also means that we will be for ever cut off from him after death for eternity. When you meet with God after death (and you certainly will) would you want to try to justify yourself and your life on the basis of what you have done – or not done? Or would you prefer to acknowledge, as I will do, that I have no acceptable grounds to prove I am perfect and thus able to enter into a perfect eternity. Instead I will point to the perfect solution that God himself has provided and say that I have the right to enter in because of all that Jesus has done for me. I know a just and righteous God, as well as a loving God, and I know he will not turn me away because I have accepted what he himself has provided. We all believe that some day we will die and the Bible tells us that. However, did you know that in the same breath that the Bible tells us we will die it also tells us that there will be judgement? 'Just as people are destined to die once, and after that to face judgement,.....' (Hebrews 9:27).

We have a God of love – yes indeed. But, having provided all that is necessary for us to enter into a relationship with him, surely it is fair that if we reject all that has been offered, then we accept the consequences of such a decision?

Consider for a moment that Jesus was prepared to give up his life in heaven in order to come to earth – because of his love for *you*. Consider that he lived life here – with all its problems and difficulties – because he wanted *you* to know what God was like and how much he loved *you*. Think for a moment that, as God, he knew that your sins would make it impossible for you to have a relationship with a holy God and so he died for *you*. Oh what a wonderful day it was for me, and can be for you, when I realized that the burden of sin had been lifted from me. I began to understand the great love of Jesus and was able to begin to have a relationship with him! So, I know I am able to have a relationship with God because Jesus came and because he died on the cross in order to redeem me.

However, thankfully there is much more to tell about how I know I know God because Jesus rose again!

Amazing Grace

Amazing grace! How sweet the sound
That saved a wretch like me;
I once was lost, but now am found,
Was blind, but now I see.

'Twas grace that taught my heart to fear,
And grace my fear relieved;
How precious did that grace appear,
The hour I first believed!

(John Newton)

Chapter 4
DEATH DEFEATED

"Ok, so perhaps I accept that Jesus came and died on a cross but I have heard it said that Jesus then rose from the dead. Christians talk about this particularly at Easter time. Is it true?"

"Yes of course it's true – how could it be otherwise?"

"What do you mean? He could have stayed in the tomb like all the other dead people I know about."

"Do you know why death entered our world, in the first place?"

"Can't say I have ever really thought about it. It's just one of those things you know. We are born and we live for a few years and then we die. It's just how it is."

"The reason death came in was because of sin."

"What? You mean it's Adam's fault?!"

"Well not really, because all men sin. The wages of sin is death. If there were no sin there would be no death. In the beginning, before Adam sinned, he could have eaten the fruit from the tree of life and then would have lived for ever. Instead he disobeyed God and took fruit from the only tree that he had forbidden him to touch."

"That does sound a bit like me. I would have done just the same! I always have a preference to do what I am told not to do –a bit like children really!"

"So because Adam sinned, God had to make sure he was unable to reach the tree of life because it would have been terrible if man, in sin, could live for ever."

"Well I can certainly see that. When you see all the dreadful things happening in the world and you see the sickness and suffering, it would be awful to live for ever with that."

"So, to get back to where we were – death is a consequence of sin. That is why Jesus rose again. Death could not hold him, death had no power over him because he was perfect. He was the only one who could defeat death because he was the only man who never sinned. He was able to take on the sin of the world because he was perfect and he was able to defeat death, because he was perfect."

"Oh I think I can see what you mean now when you said it could not be otherwise. He could not possibly stay in the grip of death because death is a consequence of sin and therefore it had no hold on him. What does that mean for me though? If death has been defeated do I still have to die?"

"Yes indeed because death is the consequence of sin and everyone sins. That is why the Bible says that everyone is destined to die - (Hebrews 9:27)."

"So if I have to die – and I can understand why – how can you say that death has been defeated?"

"The sting of death has been taken away, (see 1 Corinthians 15: 54 - 55), so that you do not need to fear death anymore. If you know Jesus then he will be with you right through death and then you will be with him for ever – you will have eternal life."

"Wow! Will I still be me, if you know what I mean?"

"Yes indeed, your spirit, your identity, will remain although you will have a different body."

"That sounds a bit scary."

"Why should it? The idea is demonstrated all the time in what we call nature. Look at the way a butterfly comes from a chrysalis. Look how a seed falls from a plant that dies and then becomes another, but different, beautiful plant - (see 1 Corinthians 15: 35 – 56)."

"Now you put it like that I think I can remember reading in the Bible somewhere where Jesus speaks about his death, comparing it with a kernel of wheat dying - (John 12:24). He says that if it dies it produces many seeds or something like that."

"Yes and this is another way in which death has been defeated. It is no longer the end but the beginning! Because Jesus died there will be 'much fruit', in other words millions and millions of people – a countless number - populating heaven. In the meantime there are millions of people throughout time who have enjoyed, and are enjoying, a relationship with God while on earth. This is all possible because not only did Jesus die but he rose again."

"That is brilliant because if Jesus rose again and death could not hold him it must mean he is still alive today and that is why I can have a relationship with him."

"I think we are getting somewhere!"

Because Jesus was sinless, it meant that death could not hold him. It had no power over him. God has decreed that the 'wages of sin is death' (Romans 6:23), which is why each of us, at some time, must die. We each have a terminal illness – the result of sin, and this means that one day we will die. But Jesus was the only man to whom this did not apply and as a result death could not hold him and he rose again. He defeated the power of sin and the power of death and was able then to return to the place which is rightfully his – at the right hand of God. Another reason why it is possible for me to have a relationship with God!

Jesus defeats death

If Jesus had not risen again and if he had been defeated by death then it would be impossible for me to have a relationship with God. A just, holy, righteous God – how could he have a relationship with sinful humanity? We little understand how terrible sin is in the sight of God. He could not possibly have a relationship with man unless the question of sin had been resolved. Maybe you think, as I have thought, but why did Jesus have to die before he rose again? Surely he could have come to earth and lived here and then just gone back to heaven again. As he is God, then surely he could have just gone to heaven without having to go through death? Yes indeed, he could have done this but then where would that leave you and me?

If Jesus had done this, then we would never have been able to know God and to have a relationship with him. We would have been excluded from heaven and an eternity with God. Death would have been exactly that – death with no hope. Yes we would have been able to see what God was like, by learning about Jesus and his life on earth, but that would have been all. We would have had no way of bridging the gap between us and God – Creator and created, the Holy One and sinners. We would have had to die because of our sin but we could not then have enjoyed life after death. We would have had to stand on our own merits and our own supposed righteousness before God and accept the just punishment. How awful and how awesome to be able to see the wonder and perfection of God from a vast distance but never to be able to enter into a relationship with him. I believe there are many religions which talk about God but because the Lord Jesus is rejected there is never a way to have a personal relationship with him.

And so just as Adam was the first man to exist and then died, so we must die. Adam is known as the 'first man' in the Bible. However, because Jesus died and rose again so we also can die and rise again and this is why Jesus is known as the 'second man' – 'The first man was of the dust of the earth; the second man is of heaven' (1 Corinthians 15:47). Why should it be so strange that after death we will be given a heavenly body? Nature points to this concept all the time. When the farmer sows a seed it does not come to life in its final form unless it first dies. An acorn becomes an oak tree and seed becomes wheat. There are different kinds of flesh too – humans have one kind of flesh or body, and animals have another, fish have another and so on. Why is it so strange to think that our bodies can, and will, be changed into heavenly ones? Maybe you wonder what this would be like and so do I. God has not seen fit to explain exactly how this will happen and what we will be like, probably because we would not understand the detail anyway! Nevertheless, God had a plan since the beginning of creation that the first order would be superseded by the second order and I am so thankful that he did!

The resurrection

You probably believe that Jesus did live on this earth. History records this fact as it does the life and death of many other people. I expect you know that it is not just the Bible that tells us that Jesus lived on earth. Even the crucifixion of Jesus is recorded in history books – those history books that you would normally read and not for a moment would you question their accuracy. That part of Christianity is not difficult to believe. The problem for most people though is that they have difficulty believing that Jesus rose from the dead and is now alive. This requires faith, of course, and we will be looking at this later in this book. However, for the moment I would like you to consider some other points about the resurrection of Jesus which help us to know this actually happened.

First of all, there is the empty tomb to consider and then the many examples of Jesus appearing to various people when he had risen from the dead. These were people like tax gatherers and fishermen and they were men who would later die, in fact they were martyred, because they believed that Jesus has risen from the dead. They obviously actually believed they had seen Jesus after he had risen from the dead. Someone has said to me that they probably imagined it. Well, apart from the fact that these were not really the type of people who would be prone to imagine things there is also a record of Jesus having appeared to over 500 people. Would they all have imagined it?

Secondly, what about the growth of the church? Following the word-of-mouth witness to all they had seen and heard by those early followers of Jesus, the church began to grow and has continued to grow until this day.

Everlasting life

So because Jesus died and rose again he has made it possible for me to have life after death. Jesus says, 'I am the resurrection and the life. The one who believes in me will live, even though they die; and whoever lives by believing in me will never die' (John 11:25-26). When I die I know that my spirit, that which is essentially me, will go to be with Jesus and this is what he means when he says that if I believe in him I will not die. I will pass through death to everlasting life – how wonderful – but in the meantime there is a life here to be lived, in relationship with him, trying to do what he wants me to do.

Of course I accept that you can easily dismiss these things as untrue or even irrelevant. In fact, you will have to do so or you may find you have to give what I am saying some serious thought and attention! What you cannot dismiss however is the experience of millions of people throughout history to the present day. Many millions of Christians would be able to talk to you about their true and daily experience of having a relationship with a living Jesus. They know, and I know, that we know God because we have a relationship with him.

As I have said, in order to experience these things we need the God-given gift of faith, so let's look at this in our next chapter.

Amazing Grace

When we've been there ten thousand years..
Bright shining as the sun.
We've no less days to sing God's praise…
Than when we first begun.

Amazing grace! How sweet the sound;
That saved a wretch like me;
I once was lost but now am found,
Was blind, but now I see.

(John Newton)

Chapter 5
FAITH

"I would like to believe in God but how can I do that when I don't believe he exists, if you know what I mean?'"

"Yes, I do know what you mean – you can't exactly make yourself believe what you don't believe can you?"

"No, but if God does exist then I do want to know that."

"You need faith. Without faith it is impossible to know God."

"What is faith?"

"That's a big question but it includes believing in something you can't see."

"That sounds crazy."

"Why? You do it all the time."

"How?"

"Well, you believe you have air around you but you can't see it. You believe in the power of electricity but you can't see it."

"Oh yes, I suppose I do. But that's because I can see the effect it is having. There is something I can see – the effect – because the air is there."

"A bit like creation then? You can't see God but you can see the effect that he is here – all around you every day – the birds, the trees, the mountains, the sea, the beautiful sunset that he sometimes paints, the stormy sea that he sometimes stirs up and so on.'"

"Oh yes, well..... I thought they just sort of 'happened', you know, by chance or accident or the laws of nature or something."

"A bit like electricity just happening or something like that?"

"Hmm, can we change the subject and get back to faith? I have heard about people having faith in God, and you seem to have it, but how do I get it?"

"Faith is a gift from God – like so many other gifts that are available for you, if you really want them."

"What else is on offer?"

"Forgiveness of your sins, the gift of the Holy Spirit, peace, joy, justification, sanctification, redemption."

"Stop, stop, I can't take that all in and I don't even understand half the words. Let's just concentrate on faith for the moment – how do I get that?"

"Ask God for it."

"That's ridiculous. How can I even talk to him if I don't believe in him?"

"Try it."

And that is exactly what I did when I was struggling to believe! I remember it well. I was envious of other Christians who seemed to have such great faith. Why did I not have their conviction and their faith? I actually wanted to believe but I just couldn't. I remember speaking to God and telling him that I really didn't believe he was there. I poured out my heart and pleaded with him, that if he was really there, then to show me the reality of his presence. I was struggling to believe and I wanted to believe but I found I was unable to do so.

Asking for faith

Many days and nights I had struggled with this problem before I finally thought that the best thing to do was to ask God for faith. I reasoned that if he was there and he was listening to me then surely he would answer me. And so I asked him. What happened next? Flashing lights and earthquakes? A voice from the sky saying, 'Here is faith'? No, I am sorry to tell you, none of that happened. In fact, nothing appeared to happen at all!

Yes I was very disappointed, very sad, even angry, that there seemed to be silence after my impassioned plea. Life continued much as before for some time. However, the fact I am now writing this book tells the final story, or perhaps I should not say the final story as I am certain I have so much more to learn. Yes, God has given me faith and my prayer was answered. Not when and how I wanted it to be but certainly answered. Furthermore, I am now sure that although it was not *my* timing, it was the best timing, although it was not *my* way, it was the best way and God gave me faith – how else could I have received it? Then, after faith, comes understanding. It is from the perspective of faith that everything begins to make sense and I begin to understand much that before simply made no sense at all.

Faith brings us all down to the same level irrespective of intelligence, circumstances or anything else. The most ignorant can enjoy a relationship with God as can the most intelligent – although the latter sometimes finds this more difficult.

The Bible tells us that, 'you will find him if you seek him with all your heart and with all your soul' – (Deuteronomy 4 v 29). We cannot be casual or half-hearted about God. He does not leave that option open to us. We can either accept him or reject him, there are no half-measures. He has said that if you seek him you will find him *but* it has to be with all your heart and soul. Notice that the Scripture does *not* say here 'with all your understanding'. When we first come to know God it has to be on the basis of a deep desire in our heart to find him. We have to put aside our so-called wisdom and intelligence and seek him with all our *heart*. If we try to find him through logic and reason we will fail miserably. God is too great and too far above our understanding to be limited by mere human reason, so we have to put that aside as we seek him. Of course, when we know him, then he often opens our minds and our understanding and things fall into the right place and begin to make sense - but only when we are guided by him. First though, it is a matter of the heart.

Anselm of Canterbury said, 'I do not seek to understand in order that I may believe, but I believe in order to understand'. He then goes on to say, 'For I believe this; unless I believe I will not understand'[4]. In other words, it has to start with faith and only then comes understanding. It doesn't work the other way round! But, you may ask, how can I manufacture such an earnest desire to know God? Well, *you* cannot but God can! You cannot manufacture desire in your own strength but you *can* ask God for this desire. You may have to ask him, first of all, for the desire to seek him just as I had to do.

Perhaps the subject of faith should have been at the very start of the book because without faith it is impossible to please God and therefore impossible to have a relationship with him. The Scripture says, 'And without faith it is impossible to please God, because anyone who comes to him must believe that he exists, and that he rewards those who earnestly seek him' (Hebrews 11:6). We are told elsewhere in the bible (Ephesians 2:8) that faith is a gift from God, so we cannot obtain it by our own endeavours.

Christianity is based on faith, not reason, and we must always keep this in mind. Why should that be? Because it was part of God's plan that this should be so. It is a great equalizer and as I have already said it is open to the rich and the poor, it is open to the educated and the uneducated. You don't have to be able to read to have faith; you don't have to have money to have faith; you can live in a slum or a palace and you can still have faith. What a wise and good God we have! So we need faith because this is how God has planned it and if we won't accept Christianity on God's terms then what we accept is not Christianity at all but some 'religion' of our own making. If we are to have a relationship with God it has to be on his terms and we have to accept the way that he has provided for us to know him.

You may think you only have a little faith but that is not the point. My faith is only small but it is in Someone who is mighty! This means that any experience I have as a result of faith is not down to my faith but down to God's power. Having said that, faith does lead to experience and that, in turn, increases my confidence in God and in the reality of my faith. Faith also needs to be used. If I have a little faith and use it, then God steps in to confirm it and thus my faith grows. The trouble with many of us is that we are sometimes afraid to step out in faith and thus we miss the wonderful opportunity of God showing his power in our lives in order to confirm that faith.

Proving God exists

I have often been told, 'you can't prove God exists'. Of course, I cannot prove the existence of God as some would understand 'proof'. Where there is no faith then anything that happens or exists will always have another explanation. It will be coincidence, or it will be science, or nature, or in the case of miracles it will be illusion, or acting. There will always be another reason so as not to accept that God exists and that he wants to be in a relationship with me.

If I look back over my life I could speak of hundreds of examples which come immediately to mind where God has acted in my life. If I tell you these then if you have faith you will understand exactly what I mean. If however you do not have faith you will probably say on each occasion, 'Oh, what a coincidence' or 'well that would probably have happened anyway'! Anything is better than believing that God has worked, and is working, in my life! Is it really easier to believe in hundreds of 'coincidences' than it is to have faith in God?

I have been accused of having a 'blind' faith and such an accusation springs from a lack of understanding. It is faith that allows me to see. Before I had faith, I was blind. Blind to the existence of God; blind to the wonder of creation; blind as to my sin and, of course, because I was blind, I could not see any reason that I needed a remedy for that sin. It is faith that helps us see and faith that gives us understanding - a faith that is based on fact. It is a fact that humankind exist and live on planet earth. It is a fact that Jesus came to earth even if we do not accept the reason he came. It is a fact that the Bible exists and has done so for about 2000 years. These facts should be enough to encourage any thoughtful person to at least give time and attention to asking themselves, 'What if it is true after all?' If it is true, then surely you can see there is nothing more worthwhile on which to spend your time. If it is not true, then surely you need to be totally convinced of that because of the consequences if you find you are wrong.

So, as to the proof of the existence of God, once faith is at work there are numerous pointers to his existence for those who have the eyes to see. Not a single blade of grass can produce itself. Man in all his supposed wisdom cannot ever create something from nothing. There must always be something there in the first instance for man to work with. Man has to start with something and then develop it – he cannot ever make anything from nothing, only God can do that and call forth the creation.

Charles Spurgeon rightly said, "If you believe in God, it is easy to see God everywhere – in the stones, in the rocks, in the rippling brooks. It is easy to hear him everywhere – in the lowing of cattle, in the rolling of thunders and in the fury of tempests. Christ is to me the wisdom of God. I can learn everything now that I know the science of Christ crucified."[5]

There are the things we see around us, there are the experiences we have in our own lives, there are the times when God speaks clearly to us and most of all, there is the death of Jesus on the cross. A fact recorded in history, not just the Bible, that Jesus died on the cross. Faith accepts that he came to earth and he died for *me* and this in itself should be the only proof I require that God exists.

Faith and the Bible

As I have already said, perhaps even before faith there must be a desire to know God, an earnest desire to seek out the truth of whether he exists. The Bible tells us that those who draw near to God must believe that he exists. So how do I get faith? It comes from God alone and if you really desire it then I suggest you ask God for it!

So is there nothing for me to do except to ask God? The answer is that you cannot have faith except as a gift from God, but yes, there is something you can do while you are waiting for his answer. You can take a look at the Bible. We will be looking at the Bible in chapter 7 and will look at this issue of faith again within that context. However, suffice to say here that the Bible tells us that 'faith comes from hearing the message, and the message is heard through the word about Christ' – (Romans 10:17). In order to increase my faith and in order to hear God speaking I should read the

Bible. This is the way in which God has spoken to me on many occasions. So, yes we ask God for faith, but we also start to read the Bible. If you don't know where to start then I suggest the gospel of John. I know many people who have come to know Jesus as their Saviour and have been brought into a relationship with God when reading the gospel of John. Try it – you might again be surprised!

Radio[6]

If radio's slim fingers
Can pluck a melody
From the night and toss it over
A continent or sea;
If the petalled white notes
Of a violin
Are blown across a mountain
Or a city's din;
If songs, like crimson roses,
Are culled from thin blue air;
Why should mortals wonder
If God hears prayer?

(Ethel Romig Fuller)

Chapter 6
POWER FROM ON HIGH

"OK, so maybe I do believe there might be something in it all."

"Perhaps we're getting somewhere!"

"But say I do believe in God, a little, I still can't see how I can possibly have a relationship with him. After all, he is so great and if he designed and created the universe then how can a little creature like me, so small and insignificant, have a relationship with someone like God, so great and so powerful. It just doesn't make sense and even though I can just about understand Jesus I still don't see how I can be in a relationship with God."

'"How do you have a relationship with your wife or husband, your brother, sister, child, neighbour or anyone on earth?"

"Well, that's different because we are all human and on a similar level and think along similar lines – (although I do sometimes think some of them are on a different planet to me!) – we all have a human personality and so can relate to one another."

"Exactly. That is why God has given us the wonderful gift of his Holy Spirit."

"That means nothing to me. I don't even understand what you are trying to say."

"Well, you have a spirit don't you. The essence of who you are, your personality and what makes you, you. So, in order for man to understand more about God and to enable us to have a relationship with him, he has given the gift of his Holy Spirit to those who believe in the Lord Jesus and accept what he has done for them ."

"I didn't know that I could have such a gift."

"Well, like any gift you have to accept it. If you accept Jesus as your Saviour and thank him for all he has done for you and if you ask for the gift of the Holy Spirit then God is only too pleased to give it. It is only when you have this precious gift that you can have a relationship with God. Because it is *his* Holy Spirit – the Spirit of Jesus - he enables you to have a relationship with God."

"Yes that does make sense. I am human and God is not, so in myself I don't have the ability to have a relationship with him. However, if he gives me his Holy Spirit, the Spirit of Christ, then that would obviously give me the ability and the power to have a relationship with him. I would like that"

"God loves to give this gift to those who love Jesus but once you have received such a wonderful gift, you will have to learn to treat him properly - the Holy Spirit is God too you know."

"What do you mean by that?"

"Well, the Holy Spirit is gentle and not pushy. He will only be as free in you as you allow him to be. If you are forever wanting your own way and your own will and still want to behave in the same way you always have, then there will not be much effect in your life from his presence."

"Oh I think I can see what you mean. If my spirit and my will are always in the forefront then I won't leave much room for the Holy Spirit to take over and shape my life?"

"Yes that's exactly it. In order to allow *him* to increase in power and effect in your life, *you* have to decrease – and that's not very easy!"

"Hmmm you can say that again. I do like having my own way but I don't always like myself and what I do!"

"I'm not surprised about that! I don't like some of what I do and say either!"

"So how can I allow the Holy Spirit to work more in my life?"

"Well, if you do things that please him, like reading your Bible and speaking with God then that's a good start. Then you can speak with him and tell him you do want to give him more room. Then when he becomes more at home in you, you will find that others will notice a change in you."

"What sort of change?"

"A change for the better of course. You will start to display what is called the 'fruit of the Spirit' which is love, joy, peace, patience, kindness, goodness, faithfulness, gentleness and self-control – (see Galatians 5: 22-23)."

"Sounds lovely and it's the sort of characteristics displayed by Jesus– but doesn't sound much like me!"

"It takes time. All the while you are on earth you are a work in progress but remember that it is God's work so it all depends on him anyway and he won't let you down. If he begins something he always completes it!"

I cannot know God except in the power of the Holy Spirit. God has revealed himself to us in Father, Son and Holy Spirit. He makes himself known as my Father, I can know him because of the work and person of the Lord Jesus Christ, and I have the power and ability to know him because I have the Holy Spirit dwelling in me. If we attempt to have a relationship with God without the Holy Spirit we will find it impossible.

New Birth
What, or who, is the Holy Spirit? He is part of the Trinity or Godhead, God himself. I have a spirit, which is the essence of who I am. The Spirit of God is the very nature of God and he has been given as a gift to all those who know God through Jesus. The Bible tells us that the fruit of the Spirit is love, joy, peace, patience, kindness, goodness, fidelity (or faithfulness), meekness (or gentleness) and self-control (Galatians 5:22-23). If I allow the Holy

Spirit to work in me then I will develop these traits. You will say, I'm sure, 'I don't see much evidence of those traits in you'! That is because I don't allow the Holy Spirit to work in me as I should, I am too busy allowing my own personality and characteristics to dominate! The Holy Spirit never forces us into submission. He will never push to dominate. He waits to be invited and given space. He is likened in the Bible to a dove – gentle and easily pushed aside. As always, God gives us a choice – it is my decision whether to allow the Holy Spirit to work or not.

It is in the power of the Holy Spirit that things become new. So, if I have received the gift of the Holy Spirit then I have become, what the Bible calls, a new creation. I have a new birth and I have been born again. We hear sometimes about 'born again' Christians as if this is some special class. The truth is that if we have received the gift of the Holy Spirit then we are born again. If I have this power and ability within me, supplied by the Holy Spirit, then I am born again, I am a new creation. So if I am truly a Christian, in other words, if I have a relationship with God, then I am born again. It is not a separate class of people within a particular religion, it is what God desires for each one of us. God wants to have a relationship with you so he has provided the way for this to be possible and then he has supplied the power that you need for it.

I have said that the Holy Spirit makes things new and he also gives us the ability to keep the *new* commandment which forms the basis of the new covenant that God made with man through the coming of Jesus. The Bible tells us that the new law is based on love. Jesus says, in the Gospel of John chapter 13 verse 34, 'A new command I give you: Love one another. As I have loved you, so you must love one another.' What a standard that is – we cannot possibly hope to keep such a command in our own strength or with our own ability – we need help.

A New Nature

The Holy Spirit is also able to give us a new nature – if we allow him to work in our lives. We have seen that he is likened to a dove in the Bible to help us to understand his sensitive nature. We can easily upset, or as the Bible says 'grieve', the Holy Spirit by our behaviour. When we have received the gift of the Holy Spirit we will find that our own nature and desires often come into conflict with the Spirit. If we always insist on our own ways – selfishness, jealousy, immorality and so on - which are against his nature, we will find that he will retire into the background of our lives. If however we allow him, and ask him, to work in our lives, then we will see the result of this. I meet Christians who I aspire to be like; those who show love, joy, peace, patience, kindness, goodness, faithfulness, gentleness and self-control. These are people who allow the Holy Spirit to work in their lives and thus display, what is called in the Bible, the 'fruit of the Spirit'. In the Bible the Holy Spirit is also likened to fire, water, wind, oil and these things give the idea of power. He is the power within us to do right instead of wrong and the power to choose good rather than evil.

A friend of mine said to me once that he found it easier to believe in the devil than in God because there was so much evidence of evil in the world. I can understand why he would say that because the devil does indeed wreak havoc in the world. However, there is a power much stronger than evil which is the power of the Holy Spirit and because he dwells in men and women here on earth it means that there is a restraint on evil. One day though, those who have this wonderful gift of the Holy Spirit will be taken away from the earth to be with Christ. The Bible warns us about the terrible times there will then be on the earth when the Holy Spirit is gone. Evil will be unrestrained for a short time until God, in his mercy, steps in and conquers it finally and for ever. In the meantime, I thank God that he has given me this power from on high to help me live for him and to have a relationship with him.

My Counsellor

The Bible speaks about the Holy Spirit as a Counsellor and in many ways this title speaks for itself. If I am in trouble or confusion I can speak with the Holy Spirit and ask him to make things clear for me. We sometimes approach human counsellors in order to try and make sense of things that happen in our lives. However, the Holy Spirit is the best Counsellor we could ever find and is always ready to give help, guidance, strength and understanding whatever our circumstances. There have been times when I have poured out my heart to the Holy Spirit, trying to make sense of what is happening in my life and he has helped me to understand. I have asked him to help me as I read the Bible and don't understand certain things.

Either then, or later, I find he gives me insight and understanding about things that had previously really puzzled me. It is particularly important to ask for the guidance of the Holy Spirit when I read my Bible. The Bible is not always easy to understand and if I read it like any other book I may misunderstand the meaning. However, the Holy Spirit was the One who inspired those who wrote the different parts of the Bible and therefore if I am to understand it rightly I must seek his help.

A Conversation with a Friend

A friend of mine said to me one day that he thought he would become a follower of Jesus, not because he believed that Jesus had died for him but because Jesus had said we should love our neighbour as ourselves. My friend had decided that if we all did this then there would not be many – or indeed any - problems in the world. Well, he was right in that last thought but there is a big problem with his first comment. My poor friend did not realize – but he will – that we are not able in our own strength and power to keep that commandment effectively. The only way I am able to love my neighbour as myself, in the right way, is in the power of the Holy Spirit. I am only able to receive the gift of the Holy Spirit if I accept Jesus as my Saviour, because the Holy Spirit is the Spirit of Jesus and cannot be given if I reject him. So my friend will find that trying to do it his way just simply will not work. We cannot improve on God's plan and it is foolishness to try to do so.

So when we receive the gift of the Spirit we find that we are then on a different path. We are on a new and living way, the way that leads to a knowledge of God, a relationship with him while on earth, and a future beyond death which is eternally secure.

All these things are possible only with 'power from on high', the power of the Holy Spirit. God has given us this wonderful gift because he wants us to know him and to have a relationship with him.

I am a new creation[7]

I am a new creation
No more in condemnation
Here in the grace of God I stand.
My heart is overflowing,
My love just keeps on growing,
Here in the grace of God I stand.
A joy that knows no limit
A lightness in my spirit
Here in the grace of God I stand.

(Dave Bilbrough)

Chapter 7
RELATIONSHIPS WITH GOD

"Why do Christians make so much fuss about the Bible?"

"Well, first of all, who do you think wrote it?"

"Now that's a good question. I suppose a lot of people did. Actually when I looked for that, out of interest, on my Amazon Kindle the other day, it said 'unknown'!"

"So who do you think is the author?"

"Lots of people I suppose."

"How do you suppose they managed to get it into one coherent whole?"

"Now that's a good question. I have puzzled about that because as some of them lived hundreds of years before or after others, it would have been a bit difficult to liaise – especially when I think about the fact that technology was not the same then as it is today!"

"So there must have been an 'unseen hand' making sure it was all pulled together then?"

"I suppose so although I had never really thought about it before. Now I suppose you are going to say God was the Unseen Hand?"

"Do you remember we were speaking earlier about the Holy Spirit which God has given to those who know and love him through the Lord Jesus Christ?"

"Yes I do remember that. What is the relevance of that here though?"

"The Holy Spirit inspired lots of different people to write, as God directed them, so that there would be a written record of many things

56

that he wanted humankind to know. That is why the Bible is called the Word of God."

"Oh I see – that must be how he managed to co-ordinate everyone so that the Bible became one complete whole. That's fantastic!"

"Yes it is rather good isn't it!"

"So, if God directed the whole operation and it really is his word then I can quite see why it is special. If it is his word then I must be able to learn quite a lot about him from it."

"Yes, of course and that is why many Christians love to read it. It contains God's wisdom and a lot more besides. It has the answers to many questions in life, it is able to teach, it shows how you should live your life in the way that is absolutely best for you and for others and much much more."

"Wow, in that case I suppose I should read it a bit more – or even a bit! I suppose it also tells all about Jesus?"

"Yes indeed – from beginning to end the Bible speaks about Jesus! The Old Testament points forward to his coming and the New Testament speaks about when he actually did come to earth, his life, his death and his resurrection – as well as a lot more besides of course. It will also show you, if you read it, many examples of men and women in relationship with God – and might even convince you that you can have a relationship with God yourself."

"Sounds interesting but I just have one more problem about all this."

"What is it?"

"Well, you say it is the Word of God and I know many Christians think that too. But, I can't just make myself believe that can I? You know, it's like believing anything – you might see why it could be true but how can I actually believe that deep in my heart?"

"How about asking God to work in your heart and mind so that you do believe the Bible is the Truth and inspired by the Holy Spirit and the Word of God. Oh, and you will have to read it too you know!"

"Will that work?"

"Try it!"

That is what I did! At one time in my life I didn't think the Bible was particularly special. In fact, had I given my honest opinion during many years of my life, even after I became a Christian, I would have said it was boring. Why then has there been such a huge change in how I feel? How can a book at one time be boring and then become the most challenging, exciting, fulfilling book I have ever read? How can it change from being boring to being the book to which I turn when I'm happy, when I am distressed, when I need guidance, when I lose a loved one – in fact in just about every circumstance of my life? The answer can only be the one to which I have alluded in the above conversation – I asked God to change me and he did! I can see no other reason why or how there could have been such a change in my heart.

The First Step

First though, I had to take a step of faith and actually begin to read it! I could see others who held the Bible in such high esteem and I was curious as to why this should be. Perhaps this was the reason I spoke to God about it in the first place. I simply asked, that if this book really was special, if it really was his word, then he would give me this conviction in my heart. I then thought that perhaps at the same time I should start to read it in a more disciplined fashion than I had previously done. So I started to try and read a small section each day and very soon, to my astonishment, I actually began to enjoy it!

Now, I cannot say that I immediately had any sort of conviction about it being inspired but I did begin to enjoy reading it. When my conviction came that the Bible is inspired and is the Word of God, I really do not know. All I know is that there was a time I did not think the Bible was the Word of God and I wasn't sure if it was true. I know there was also a day when I asked God to give me a deep conviction as to whether it was actually true, whether it was inspired and whether it was his Word. I also know that today I have this deep conviction in my heart about the Bible and I know that God answered my prayer. So here is yet another illustration of the way in which I know that I know God. I spoke to him, he heard me, and he answered me and the Bible has been invaluable in helping to deepen my knowledge of God and my relationship with him.

God's desire to be in relationship with me

There is so much in the Bible and a chapter like this will not be enough to even scratch the surface but I will attempt to describe some of the wonderful things I have learned from it in order to give just a glimpse of what is available for anyone who desires it. From Genesis to Revelation God speaks to us about himself, his ways, his love, his desire to have a relationship with us, his desire for us to live our lives in the way he intends which always leads to our blessing. Any feeble attempt of mine to explain these things will always be just that, a feeble attempt, when viewed beside the personal experience which is available for you, *if* that is what you want.

Throughout the Bible God shows us he is a God of relationship. He has revealed himself to us through the Father, the Son and the Holy Spirit. A God of relationship. There are numerous examples of God having a direct relationship with man, beginning with Adam in the book of Genesis and then revealing the vision of Revelation to John on the Isle of Patmos. So, not only has God made it all possible, through the Lord Jesus Christ, but he has also given us so many examples of men and women who knew him and had a personal relationship with him.

We learn from Adam about the disastrous consequences of disobeying God. We learn there are consequences not just for ourselves but for the generations that follow. We learn that God does not force us to follow his way but allows us to make a choice. Humankind can blame no one else for the problems and sorrow in the world caused by disobeying God and by sin.

We learn from Cain that jealousy can have terrible consequences and can even lead to murder. We learn from Noah that if we are prepared to take God at his word, perhaps accepting jeers and abuse from others as a result, then not only is there a tremendous blessing for us personally, but also for our families and many more generations besides. We learn from Abraham, that God always keeps his word, even if the answers come only after we have died. We learn from Joseph (in the book of Genesis) that God is able to work out the apparent disasters in our lives for good, both for ourselves and others. Those famous words of Joseph – 'you intended to harm me but God intended it for good' (Genesis 50.20) – show how God can use bad things for our eventual blessing.

I read in Exodus of the journey of the Israelites out of Egypt and I see their relationship with God going through highs and lows – just like mine. I could go on through every book in the Bible and tell you things I have learned from it. I have found the Bible to be a living book like no other. I can read something today which means nothing personally, only to find that when I read it again several months later it has a whole new meaning and applies to a specific situation in my life. I know I am not alone in this and that millions of Christians will agree – the question is do you? If not, you have the chance to find out for yourself, whether I speak the truth, by speaking to God about such experience to discover that it is also available for you.

Jesus at the centre

I have already mentioned in chapter two that Jesus Christ is the centre and at the very heart of the Bible. It speaks of him from beginning to end. The Old Testament is an account of the nation of Israel – the nation that was established by God to bring Jesus into the world. It contains prophecy after prophecy about the coming of the Lord Jesus. The New Testament tells us about the time when Jesus did actually come, the Word becoming flesh, in order to redeem humankind. The coming of Jesus Christ into our world, the central event in history – the Old Testament sets the scene and then the New Testament describes it. There is a unity of thought throughout the Bible which must be apparent to any thoughtful reader, indicating that there must have been only one Mind which inspired those who wrote it and those who compiled it.

We are so intelligent about so much today. Our world, our entertainment, our jobs and so on, but what about becoming intelligent about the Bible? There are many people I speak to, or I read about, who have so much to say against the Bible but I wonder how many of them have actually read it! What about you? Are you afraid that if you read it you might actually believe it and find that it is possible to know God and to have a relationship with him? Are you afraid that it might condemn you? Are you afraid that your life may have to change as a result? I doubt that it is possible for you to read the Bible and find that it doesn't change you! I also know that when it does it will be an enormous change for the better and you will never ever regret it – neither during your time on earth, nor in eternity.

The Bible – the best seller

Finally, did you know that if counted as a single book, the Bible is the best selling book in history with sales estimates around 6 billion? Did you know that many of the everyday expressions you use actually come from the Bible? For example, 'a fly in the ointment' (Ecclesiaties 10.1); 'a man after my own heart' (Samuel 13.14 and Acts 13.22); 'a labour of love' (1 Thessalonians 1.3); 'a wolf in sheep's clothing' (Matthew 7.15); 'at his wit's end' (Psalms 107.27); 'the apple of his eye' (Deuteronomy 32.10 and Zechariah 2.8). These Bible references are all from the King James Version of the Bible because it is this version which has been so enormously influential in the development of the English language. There are many more examples, far too many to list here, but the point is this – if the Bible is such an important book then why does it lie gathering dust on your bookshelf – that is, if you even have one at all.

Have you ever wondered why it is that so many writers, composers, artists and other great men and women throughout history have used people, themes and inspiration from the Bible for their work? You may enjoy listening to, or watching, the results of such inspiration. You may enjoy reading the books which have been written but why then do you never take a look at the book from which this inspiration comes? Perhaps you rush to buy the books in the top-sellers list today – you may spend hours reading other books or watching television programmes. Why not try this wonderful best seller – why not give some of your time to really read it thoroughly. It will be one of the best decisions of your life and you may even find that what I am saying is actually true after all!

The Bible is God's revelation to his people[8]

'When we talk about Christianity being true the unchurched person of today shrugs with disinterest. 'You have your truth, I have mine.' What he wants to know is, 'Does it work?'…..

The God of the Bible offers us supernatural wisdom and assistance in our struggles, difficulties, and recovery from past hurts. But we need to communicate that the reason it works is because it's *true.* ….

And because the Bible is God's revelation to his people, it contains a kind of practical and effective help that's unmatched by mere human philosophers….

As far as Christianity is concerned, we're not saying it's true because it works; we're saying Christianity is true and therefore it works.'

(Lee Strobel)

Chapter 8
REVELATION

"You must understand why I find it so difficult to believe in God."

"What do you mean?"

"Well, there is no proof he exists and if he is there why doesn't he reveal himself. I know we have talked about the creation but if I dismiss that with some other theory, (even though you think such theories are false), then what else is there? "

"Do you accept that you can never fully understand God?"

"Yes, I suppose I do. If I believed in him then he would have to be so great that I'm sure I could never understand him."

"You are certainly right there. You may not know this but the Bible speaks about the potter and the clay to give us an example of this. The clay will never fully understand the potter although it has been formed and made by him."

"Yes but where does that leave me in trying to understand the whole concept of God?"

"If you accept that you could never understand God then what would be the best way for him to reveal himself to you?"

"Now that is a difficult one. I suppose he would have to come down to my level – ah yes, we have talked about that. God has already done that in Jesus – God with us – the Word become flesh in the second chapter. Is there anything else?"

"What about giving you the ability to know him?"

"Ah yes, we covered that when we talked about the gift of the Holy Spirit."

"And there is something else. What do you hear people often speak about when they speak about Jesus, the Son, and the Holy Spirit?"

"Ummm – hey I think I know that! We speak about the Father, the Son and the Holy Spirit."

"Yes that's right. God has revealed himself in the Father, the Son and the Holy Spirit! We haven't spoken much yet about God being my Father and what people mean when they speak about the Trinity. God revealed in Father, Son and Holy Spirit. I can't say I fully understand it – and especially how God has done it – but it helps me tremendously to know God in this way."

"Yes it must be pretty special to think of God as your Father."

"Yes indeed it is. You see he wants our relationship to be so close – like a parent and a child. This doesn't fully reflect his love for us of course, as human parents are always imperfect in some way, but you can understand the concept."

"Yes I think I can."

"And of course God has shown just how much he loves me because Jesus died on the cross for me. I cannot question his love after that can I!"

"No I suppose not. So what you are saying is that I can know the love of God and I can know him, to some extent, as God the Father, God the Son and God the Holy Spirit."

"Yes exactly. Now isn't that wonderful!"

God wants to be in a relationship with me! The enormity of that fact blows my mind. Indeed the easiest way to deal with it is to simply dismiss it, which I did for many years. The easiest way to deal with it is for me to say 'that's impossible' and then decide that, rather than explore it further, I will just not believe it. That is what many people decide to do. The enormity of God's plans and purposes are just too great for the human mind to encompass and therefore I, in my wisdom, prefer to say it is not true. But of course, just because I choose to say it is not true does not make one jot of difference as to whether or not it is!

God the Father, God the Son and God the Holy Spirit

Many books have been written on this subject by others who are far more able to explain these things. However, I could not write about the way that God has made it possible for me to know him without reference to the way in which he has revealed himself. God knew we could never fully understand him but he has revealed enough about himself which we can understand in order to come into relationship with him. We can understand the concept of a father because we each have a father. Obviously our own fathers are human and imperfect but even so we are able to understand, in a small way, what a perfect father might be like. We can understand a little about Jesus because he was a man like ourselves, except that he had no sin. We can also understand a little about the Holy Spirit because we each have a spirit – that which gives us our identity and our nature; that which makes me, me. What better way could there have been for God to reveal himself so that we can understand – even if imperfectly because of our limited human minds.

So when I am asked why God does not reveal himself, the answer is that he has done so. He has revealed himself in the Father, the Son and the Holy Spirit. The problem with many who ask that question though is that what they really mean is, why has God not revealed himself *in the way in which I think he ought to do so*. Instead of accepting what God has done, we think that we know a better way and we think we know what he ought to have done. If only we would come to him in humility instead of pride we would find that these words of the Bible are true, 'Ask and it will be given to you; seek and you will find; knock and the door will be opened to you' (Matthew 7:7).

Our Father in heaven

Many people, even those who do not profess to be Christians, know something about what we commonly call the 'Lord's Prayer'. It used to be taught in our schools and many know that it begins,

"Our Father in heaven", or "Our Father who art in heaven". I wonder if we ever stop to consider the wonderful privilege that can be ours of knowing God as 'Our Father'. The Bible tells us that if we do believe on the Lord Jesus and accept him as our Saviour then we have a right to become children of God. We read in the Gospel of John chapter 1 verse 12, 'Yet to all who did receive him, to those who believed in his name, he gave the right to become children of God'. God has given us a 'right' to call ourselves *his* children when we come to know Jesus! I can make this very personal and say that God has given *me* the right to call myself *his* child *because* I know Jesus as my Saviour. I am the child of a King. I have been adopted into the family of God because of all that Jesus has done for me. What a fantastic privilege - it is just too wonderful for words.

The highest and best privilege

Those who choose to seek God and who recognize the weakness of their humanity are able to receive the highest and best privilege known to man, that of having a relationship with God. The highest and best privilege by an immeasurable margin! The Bible says in 1 Corinthians 2:9 in the New King James Version:-

"Eye has not seen, nor ear heard,
Nor have entered into the heart of man
The things which God has prepared for those who love Him."

How do I know that God wants a relationship with me and how can it be possible? He has provided everything necessary! He has revealed himself in Father, Son and Holy Spirit so that, even with the frailty of my human mind, I can understand enough to enter into a relationship with him.

So as we come to the end of Part one let us reconsider the question which is the title of this book – how do I know I know God? It is because I have a relationship with him and I hope you have been convinced as you have read these chapters that it is possible to have a relationship with God. God has done everything necessary in order to make it possible for me to know him and to have a relationship with him. He has created this world in which I live and then sent his only Son to show me what God is like. The Lord Jesus then died on the cross to redeem me – save me from everything that could separate me from God and prevent me from knowing him. Jesus then rose again after he had defeated death and has thus shown the way in which I too can have life after death. Then God has provided the gift of faith in order that I can believe and the precious gift of the Holy Spirit in order to give me the ability to have a relationship with God. He has given me the Bible, the Word of God, and has revealed himself to me as a Father. I am his child, adopted into his family and I can know him as a child would know his father. God has revealed himself as Father, Son and Holy Spirit and this means I can know him and have a relationship with him.

However, understanding that it is possible to know God is not the same as actually knowing him which is the reason for Part two of this book. I want you to know the wonderful God that I know and for you to understand that if this is possible for me then it is definitely possible for you! Oh that I could explain the wonderful, personal, experience of having a relationship with him - the deeper my relationship with him becomes, the more wonderful I find him. Loving, patient, wise, just, righteous, majestic, glorious and much more besides so that my feeble words can never do him credit. If you know him already then you already understand this but if you don't then I long for you to have a relationship with him yourself, my reader and friend. There is nothing like it – absolutely nothing.

The Love of Christ[9]

'The love of Christ is not a different love from the eternal fire in the heart of God or that which flows between the three persons of the Trinity. We are loved passionately by God. The self-sacrificing love between the three persons is the joy at the centre of God. What is the response from us to such love?' – Ralph Wouldham

PART TWO

MY PERSONAL RELATIONSHIP WITH GOD

Chapter 9
SPEAKING AND LISTENING

"I just can't understand why God never seems to answer my prayers. I hear Christians talking about answered prayers and so on but it never really seems to work for me! Why doesn't he answer me?"

"He always does."

"I don't understand why you say that because it really doesn't seem like that to me."

"What do you mean when you say 'answer'? Do you mean why doesn't he do exactly what you ask him to?"

"Oh I don't really expect that you know. After all he is the God of the universe so I can't expect him to do what I say, can I! But what's the point of praying if he isn't going to listen?"

"He always hears you. Every time you speak to him, look to him, cry to him – he always hears you. Never never forget that. However you feel, whatever you think, he always hears you."

"But he doesn't always answer."

"Yes he does always answer. He does not always say yes though. In fact, in your case, maybe he hasn't been able to say yes much at all lately so I can understand you being a bit fed up."

"If he doesn't say yes then what does he say?"

"Sometimes he says no and sometimes he says wait. If you had children would you always give them exactly what they ask you for?"

"No, of course not. They don't understand, a lot of the time, what is best for them – especially when they are really young. As they get older and become a bit wiser then I expect I would be able to say yes more often. They would learn what I thought was right for them and

what I thought was wrong so they would start asking for the right things."

"Carry on – this is good."

"Oh I see – you think I am a child!"

"Yes, you are God's child and a very very precious one. He would never give you anything that was not good for you, he wants the very best for you and he gets quite sad when you get so down and upset when he says no. He wants you to understand that he loves you so much that he will work out everything, yes everything, for your very best. You have to trust that love – even when you don't understand."

"That's not easy sometimes! So the fact he is saying no to me quite a lot at the moment means that I may be asking for the wrong things."

"Or it might not be the right time for you to have them."

"Oh dear – perhaps the first thing I should have done was to ask him what he wanted for my life!"

"Not many people start there! If only they did, it would save a lot of pain and tears along the way. Just as a father (a good one) would never cause unnecessary pain or suffering for his child, so it is with God. He has a good plan for your life and if only you ask him then he will make sure everything falls into its right place."

"I do want that so I will ask him to show me the plan. I am sure it will include not having to work in this job for long, finding a husband with a good job and loads of money, being married in my twenties, having a few children, continuing to be in the same Christian group that I grew up in, (that's what he has done for all my friends) – oh, but that's what I've been asking for and he just doesn't seem to be doing anything!"

"Maybe he has a different plan to the one you have made!"

"Oh no! I'm not sure I want a different plan!"

"Well, it's up to you. As always he will not force you and you have the freewill to make your own decisions. You can go God's way or you can go your own way. However, you can't really expect him to keep saying yes to all the things you ask if they are not what are best for you, so you may find that path a difficult one."

"I suppose it may also make me a bit resentful towards God because it seems he keeps saying no to me – in fact, that seems to be happening. Oh dear, and yet I had some lovely ideas about what I wanted my future to look like. I was sure he would fall in with them! I will have to think about all this."

"That's fine. The choice is always yours. God wants your love, not your resentment. He wants your company and he wants what is absolutely best for you. I will leave it with you."

If God had answered yes to all my prayers then I would not be married to the man who is my husband today and I would not have met many of the wonderful people I have met. However, there is something of much more importance than that, more important than anything else at all. If God had answered yes to all my prayers then I would not know him as I do today. My knowledge of God would not have increased as it has done and my relationship with him would not be as it is today. So I can thank God that he has not said yes to all my prayers. This gives me faith and hope and trust for the present and the future – that when God says 'no' or when he says 'wait' it is for a purpose and it is for my blessing!

How does God speak?

So, if God answers prayer, this must mean he speaks to me and you might be thinking that if God speaks to me then *what* does he say and *how* does he say it and that is a fair question. So how does God speak? He speaks in many ways. You will have heard of the old saying that, 'actions speak louder than words' and perhaps this is a good place to start. When we think about speaking, most of us immediately associate that idea with words. However, even in human terms we speak in many ways without words. The expression on someone's face can speak to you far louder – and often more accurately – than the words they actually say. Simple words like, 'yes, I'll do it' can be said with several different expressions and convey pleasure, anger, sorrow and many other emotions. Sometimes in bereavement a friend will come and just sit with you, not necessarily saying anything at all. The simple act of being there conveys love and compassion and a willingness to help. A child may make a card for his or her mother and the love and effort that goes into making that card speaks loudly to the mother about the love of the child – sometimes when the child would find it very difficult to express how he or she feels in words. In husband and wife relationships actions are very important to express how we really feel about each other – often far more important than words. There is a reality and sincerity in actions that is sometimes not there when we use mere words.

So how does God speak? He does use words but he also uses many more things besides words which are often far more powerful.

He speaks to me through creation about his majesty and his greatness. He speaks to me about his great love shown when Jesus came to earth and then died on the cross for me. He speaks of his power in raising Jesus from the dead. He speaks of his great kindness and the fact that he loves to give good gifts by giving me the gift of the Holy Spirit and many more wonderful gifts besides. He also speaks to me on a very personal level about very personal things. Sometimes it may take years before I understand what he is saying to me but sometimes I understand immediately. Most of the time I have to admit that I am a very slow learner and often God has to speak with me many times, in many different ways before I finally get the message! I argue, in my mind and heart, even if not with actual words, about many things and I know I still have much to learn. How patient God is with me and as a result, my relationship with him becomes closer and I learn more about his love.

I expect you sometimes have similar problems to mine with your mobile phone. I can be talking quite happily and then sometimes the line breaks up and the voices become distorted. Each of us on either end of the line is still speaking quite clearly but it is no longer clear to the other person. Of course God always hears us clearly but sometimes we can have problems hearing him. Many things can get in the way of us hearing God speak to us. It could be my own preconceived ideas; my selfishness; my determination to have my own way; my carelessness; maybe I don't want to hear from God because of fear of what he might say, or it could just be that I never even think about the fact that God might want to speak to me. It is usually only with time and experience that we begin to learn to recognize the voice of God and the many ways in which he speaks.

God can use so many things and so many people to speak to me. He can speak through the Bible; he can speak through creation; he can speak through my circumstances; he can speak through the things that happen to me in my life; he can speak through other people and he can speak directly to me in my heart and soul.

The Bible speaks about the 'still small voice' (1 Kings 19:12 KJV) of God or 'the gentle whisper' (1 Kings 19:12 NIV). Only those who have experienced this will understand the reality of it. It may be a still small voice but sometimes it is as clear to me as if he had shouted loudly from heaven. Those who say that God does not speak today obviously do not have a relationship with him. God does speak today, but the question is can you hear him or even perhaps, do you want to hear him?

Even long ago where we have a record (in the Bible) of God speaking directly from 'heaven' there were different views. Some said God had spoken, some said it was an angel and some said it had thundered. So if we do not believe in God, we will always find an alternative explanation. I know many people with whom I can converse about how God speaks and what he says today, because they have similar experiences. God has given, and continues to give, clear guidelines about how we should live today but the question is do we listen and then do we obey – or do we think we know better?

What does God say?

You will already have seen in the first part of this book that God has spoken, and still speaks to me about many things. His power and creativity in Creation; his great love shown by Jesus coming to earth and dying on the cross for me; his generous nature in giving me good gifts such as faith and the gift of the Holy Spirit;

his wisdom in revealing himself as the Father, the Son and the Holy Spirit; and all that he has said, and still says, through the Bible. I would not have been able to write about these things if God, in his goodness, had not shown me them. I have had so many questions over the years – and still have many - and examples of these are shown in the conversations in this book. Sometimes they are questions that I have been asked, but often they are questions that I have asked myself.

God has answered many of my questions and there are still many that I believe he will answer one day. I have to accept that I do not always know the answers and sometimes, even when I ask God, I still do not have an answer. Maybe I will never have the answer while here on earth because of my limited intelligence, but I am sure that when I am with him eternally, I will have plenty of time to ask questions and I won't then be limited by my earthly mind!

So you will see that God, has said, and continues to say, many things. He speaks about big things but he also speaks about little things in my life. He asks me to forgive someone who has hurt me and made me bitter and I find, to my surprise, that when I do so it releases a joy in my heart that was not there before. Furthermore, I realize that my bitterness was only hurting me in any case and really had little or no effect on the other person! He speaks to me about decisions I have to make; He speaks to me with words of such comfort in times of bereavement; he lifts me up when I fall and make mistakes; he forgives me when I do stupid things which dishonour him and most of all, he speaks to me constantly about his love. These are just some examples, which together with the other examples in this book, should give you some idea of what God says. The difficulty I have is knowing when to stop when I start to think about all that God has said, and continues to say, to me!

Listening to God

My conversations with God used to be very one-sided and sometimes they still are. It was I who did all the speaking and it never really occurred to me to stop and listen to what he might have to say to me! I am still often like that. I come to God with a shopping list of what I would like, read it all out to him and then dash off again to get on with my life. Having said that, God still loves to hear from us even if we do not wait for his reply – such is his love and his patience.

However, if I am only interested in myself and not at all concerned about other things which are of interest to God, then this will obviously affect my relationship with him. In a human relationship if one person is focused only on their own needs and concerns, then this will obviously have a detrimental effect on the relationship. My selfishness will affect my relationship with God. He will speak with me, if that is what I desire, but it cannot be all on my terms. That is not the right basis for any relationship and certainly not for one with God. I wonder sometimes if I am not much more selfish in my relationship with God than I would ever think of being in my relationships with other people. I forget the basics of saying 'thank you' and 'I love you' and the importance of listening as well as talking.

One of the problems about life today is that, for many of us, we are always so busy. Often with worthwhile activities, but busy nonetheless. So if we never make time to listen to what God might be saying then it follows that we are unlikely to hear him speak. If we always have the television or the radio on and our minds engaged in what we are hearing or seeing then what opportunity do we give God to speak? Sometimes people say to me that God never speaks to them and I reply, "do you give him the chance?"

I have come to love the silence when there are no distractions and often it is at such times that God speaks to me. There is a wonder and a peace and a joy which cannot be explained in mere words which comes from spending time in the presence of God. The Psalmist talks about being in the secret or the shelter of his presence ('He that dwelleth in the secret place of the most High…..Psalm 91:1 KJV). It is a secret known only to those who have enjoyed the experience and cannot really be explained. Many of us know that when you spend time in the company of someone you love it is often a wonderful experience. Sometimes conversing and sometimes not, but simply enjoying the presence of one another. This is a very poor illustration in human terms but it is the only one that comes to mind which is anywhere near an attempt to explain what I mean about being in the presence of God. These are precious times and times when I often hear the still small voice of God.

Having said that, God also sometimes speaks in the hustle and bustle of life, or when something happens, or through another person so we have to learn to listen to God and not limit him to specific times or places. He is God and can speak to me at any time, in any place, through whoever, or whatever, he wishes to use. The deeper my relationship with him, the easier it will be to recognize and listen to his voice.

God knows every secret of my heart, every thought, every emotion and every aspect of every part of my life from beginning to end. There is nothing about me that he doesn't know. Sometimes we become very close to someone else here on earth, a father, a mother, a wife, a husband, a daughter, a son or a friend. We can sometimes have very deep relationships and attachments to one another but never so completely as a relationship with God through Jesus. Things I would never tell another person I can tell to Jesus. Actions that have hurt me too badly for human words, my actions which have hurt others, all known to Jesus and still he is ready to hear all about it, to comfort and advise and always to love me.

I have heard it said and know it to be true that, 'there is nothing I can do to make God love me more and there is nothing I can do to make God love me less'. What love – what incomprehensible, unexplainable love! And so there have been discussions, challenges, rebukes and exhortations which I would never want to tell another person on earth. Parts of my life known only to myself and God. Indeed I would go further and say parts of my life known only to God because he knows me better even than I know myself. What a basis for a relationship! I have such joy in this knowledge and the fact that, even knowing all the worst things about me, he still loves me! The Bible says that 'while we were still sinners Christ died for us' (Romans 5:8). He knew all about me and all about my behaviour and yet still he loved me enough to die for me.

When I am up or when I am down, tired or angry, joyful or depressed – whatever my mood or however I feel I can come to him. Always ready to listen, always ready to help – to encourage, to comfort, to challenge, to rebuke, to advise or just to hear me out – always always there and he never never fails. Why would I not want such a relationship with such a person? Sometimes speaking obliquely, sometimes directly, sometimes through a friend, sometimes through creation – God speaks in so many ways and cannot be limited. The more I know of God the more I want to know and the little I feel I do know. There are challenges and difficult times in this relationship as you will see as you read on, but that is because it is a *real* relationship which is how I know that I know God!

My Life

My life is but a weaving
Between my Lord and me
I cannot choose the colours
But He works steadily.
Often He weaves in sorrow
And I, in foolish pride,
Forget He sees the upper,
And I the under side.

Not 'til the loom is silent
And the shuttles cease to fly
Shall God unroll the canvas
And explain the reason why.
The dark threads are as needful
In the Weaver's skilful hand
As the threads of gold and silver
In the pattern He has planned.
He knows, He loves, He cares
Nothing this truth can dim.
He gives His very best to those
Who leave the choice with Him.

(Author unknown)

Chapter 10
FREEDOM TO BE ME

"Why is there so much trouble in the world?"

"You mean wars and fighting and hatred – that sort of thing?"

"Yes I do – and even things that are not as extreme as that – meanness and unfaithfulness and so on."

"You mean that humans – including you – don't always say and do right things?"

"Yes I suppose I do mean that – when God created humankind why didn't he make us so that we always make right choices?"

"God gave you freewill. The freedom to choose how to live, what to say and what to do."

"Why on earth did he do that? It hasn't worked out very well has it?"

"He wanted you to have the freedom to choose whether you wanted his company or not. He wants you to choose to love him freely. If he forced that decision it wouldn't be worth much would it?"

"No I suppose not. In fact, if love is forced I even wonder if it can be called love."

"Exactly. He has demonstrated his love for you and he has shown you how much he wants to have a relationship with you but the choice is yours."

"I can understand that a little I think – but there is a high cost factor to freewill isn't there – as I said earlier, it hasn't worked out very well has it?"

"In some ways I can see why you say that and I am sure it saddens God to see so much suffering in the world as a result of people making bad choices. However, we haven't come to the end of the story yet."

"What do you mean by that?"

"Well, do you remember hearing the story about Noah's Ark?"

"Yes yes I know that kids' story but what has that got to do with what we are talking about?"

"Actually it is not a kids' story (although children do enjoy it) it is a serious event which happened as a result of humankind making bad choices, in other words sinning."

"Really? I had never really thought about it as more than a story."

"Did you know that in the Bible it says that, 'The Lord regretted that he had made human beings on the earth, and his heart was deeply troubled.'? – (Genesis 6:6). There was so much evil in the world and humankind was behaving in such a terrible way that he had to do something."

"God sent a flood because of that? I can't believe that I never knew that before!"

"Yes he sent a flood as judgement on the evil in the world and to destroy it – except for Noah and his family as I expect you know."

"Yes I did know about Noah but I didn't know why all that happened. It was a way to start again – what we talk about as a fresh start, wiping the slate clean, that sort of thing?"

"Yes that's right and a day is coming when God will have to act again."

"Not another flood?"

"No, he has promised never to do that again - (by the way, did you know that's what the rainbow means? The Bible tells us it is a sign of God's promise never to flood the earth again as he did in the days of Noah.)

"So if he has promised not to do that again then what will he do?"

"He will bring judgement on the evil in the world by fire next time. You can read about it in your Bible. God will not always be patient although at the moment he is still waiting for us to listen to him. As you know he loves each person and would love for each one to know him and come into a relationship with him but each person has a choice and one day time will run out."

"That sounds very serious."

"It is serious and is not often spoken about today but it is very clear in the Bible. God would not be righteous if he did not eventually deal with evil. He will deal with it and it will be put away for ever."

"That sounds wonderful – things will be perfect then will they?"

"Yes indeed, there will be a new heaven and a new earth and righteousness, not sin, will be in control. The Bible says 'But in keeping with his promise we are looking forward to a new heaven and a new earth, where righteousness dwells.' (2 Peter 3:13) Those who have accepted Jesus and all that he has done for them will be able to spend eternity with him where there will be no more sin. That means no more death, no more sorrow, no more tears and so on."

"That sounds so wonderful and I'd like to be there."

"If you know and love the Lord Jesus then you will be there."

"But what about those who refuse to accept what Jesus has done and don't want to know God?"

"They will have to accept the consequences of that choice. They choose not to have a relationship with God in time and so sadly they will not have a relationship with him in eternity. Such people will be judged and will have to accept the punishment for their sin themselves. If they have rejected Jesus and what he has done for them there is no alternative. The choice is theirs."

That sounds very serious doesn't it? And of course it is. There is a serious side to what we call the 'gospel' or the good news about Jesus Christ. We have already covered the subject of the sacrifice of Jesus on the cross earlier in the book but I make no apology for coming back to it again. In my relationship with God I am brought back to the cross of Jesus time and time again. I would not want it any other way.

The highest truth
There is no higher truth than the fact that Jesus died on the cross for the redemption of humankind. God created us and then redeemed us and so I suppose we could say we belong to him twice over!

The early Christians had to contend with a religious sect known as 'Gnosticism'. One of the characteristics of Gnosticism was to attempt to gain more and more knowledge. There were different levels of attainment of knowledge and the Gnostic would strive to rise higher and higher up these levels. There are still many in religious circles, including Christian ones unfortunately, who think that they too must strive to do this. If you know in your heart, by faith, that Jesus died on the cross because of your sin, and if you accept this and thank him for it, then you have it all! There is no need to spend your life trying to attain to a higher level of knowledge. Of course as we enter into a relationship with God we find we want to know more about him and we want to understand his Word, but the foundation and the cornerstone of Christianity is Jesus Christ, and him crucified. You do not progress to a 'higher level of truth' as some might think.

I do, however, deepen in my love for him and I do deepen in my understanding of that wonderful love he has for me. Even so, I do not believe I will ever fully understand such love. It is beyond my comprehension that such a man – who is God himself – would love me so much that he would be prepared to go to such lengths for me. This is yet another wonderful aspect of my relationship with God. Always learning more but never reaching a level of perfect understanding. Day after day learning lessons and reaching some understanding of things that once were so unclear. At the same time, day after day, reaching a greater understanding that the more I learn about God the more I realize the little I know! He is ever beyond us and yet is willing to come so close to us. 'As the heavens are higher than the earth, so are my ways higher than your ways and my thoughts than your thoughts.' (Isaiah 55:9)

Free to choose

Perhaps as you would expect, another example of how I know I know God comes in again here under the subject of freewill. For a long time I could not understand why God allowed such awful things to happen. If he is so powerful, I reasoned, then why did he not just step in and stop certain things happening? But then as I spoke with him about this over the years (yes, I am afraid I am a very slow learner) I gradually began to understand a little. If he stepped in as I thought he should, then at what point should he do this and in what type of events? Let's take a war for example. Step in just as the first shot was fired? Step in just when the decision for war was being taken? Step in and allow the war but make sure no one gets hurt? Work in the heart and mind of those responsible for making the decision in the first place? Ah, now we might be getting a bit closer here because, of course, that is the answer. The heart and mind of humankind needs to be changed.

But let's continue the theme for a moment and switch to the minor wrongs. Minor perhaps in our eyes but not in God's eyes. Do you know that he is so wonderful that the Bible says his eyes are too pure even to look on evil? 'Your eyes are too pure to look on evil; you cannot tolerate wrongdoing. Why then do you tolerate the treacherous? Why are you silent while the wicked swallow up those more righteous than themselves?' (Habakkuk 1:13). So, in that case, should he step in when you want to do something which you know is wrong? Something which you are aware is greedy, selfish or just plain nasty? How many times would he have to step in then in your life? How many times a month, a week, a day? There are times in my life when, he would have been stepping in continuously as I made wrong decisions and did things about which I am now very ashamed.

If God steps in at all, then he would surely have to step in on every occasion when a wrong was committed. Perhaps you are thinking, no, no, that's daft – only on the occasions when I think it is necessary. Yes that is exactly how I thought. After endless conversations with God on this subject I realized that I was trying to take on his role! I realized that in my arrogant thinking I was prepared to say when and how God should act – often in judgement of course – on everyone else except, of course, me! If I expect him to stop sin whenever it occurs then surely I have to start with myself! Now that is a different story altogether and I am not very keen about that.

So God allows us all to make our own decisions. We can either do that in consultation with him or not. During much of my life I have made decisions and then asked God to give them his approval! To my surprise, he often has not done so! My desire now though is to ask him first. This is not easy as so often I have such firm ideas about how and what things should be done. Thankfully, he is ever patient with me and as I stumble along with him holding my hand, I know I will eventually make it because he has said, 'Never will I leave you; never will I forsake you' (Hebrews 13:5).

Free to love

I hope you can see then that if God has given us freewill then surely he will allow us to exercise it, *even when it is to our own detriment.* In this way we can choose to freely love him and we are free to choose to have a relationship with him. If we do this, then everything else falls into place. We begin to understand things that we never did before and we find that even when we do make bad decisions (which we still do!) then he is still able to use them for our blessing! I have countless examples of God doing this in my life, most of which are too personal to share here or which involve other people.

I have been told that God must be 'over indulgent' to allow us to do all that we want but he has only been so, if you call it that, in the sense that he has given us free-will. We could and can choose to live as he tells us, or we can choose not to do so. If a child, who has become an adult, makes a 'wrong' choice, in your opinion, do you (or indeed can you) stop him? You might advise, but he makes his own decisions and has to live with the consequences of those decisions. So it is with God. He does advise but it is me who makes the choice. The difference is, of course, that you cannot always stop your child doing what he chooses to do but God could stop us. He chooses, most of the time, not to do so. He has made us and given us the freedom to choose. We are not automatons and he did not want automatons who are directed by the flick of a switch. He made us in 'his image' in that we have minds and reason and can make choices about how we live. How sad that so often we choose the wrong way.

God wants me to choose to love him freely. How often we read of dictators who force their subjects to bow to them and obey them. They operate in a climate of fear and regulation but how different things are in the kingdom of God. He wants us to choose to love him and then because of that love to do his will. To do what he wants us to do, which is always for our eventual blessing. I am convinced that the more I understand about God's love for me, the more I would be willing to show that love to others in the things that I do and the things that I say. That is such a challenge even as I write it. I have been writing about the troubles in the world but if each of us was prepared to submit to God and his will in our lives there would be no more trouble. If each of us could 'love the Lord your God with all your heart' and if each of us could 'love your neighbour as yourself' (Matthew 22:37-40), there would be no need for so many rules and regulations and there would certainly be no more war.

I hear people say that religion causes wars and yes it probably does. However, if each of us had a relationship with God through Jesus Christ and was willing to submit to him and to his ways, then whether we called that 'religion' or whatever we called it, there would be no more war.

Free to be Me

As to freewill, I thank God that he has given me freewill. He allows me to be me within our relationship whilst at the same time working in me to change me. I have heard it said that, 'God loves me just as I am, but he loves me too much to leave me just as I am'! If we allow him to work with us then he will change us to become more like Jesus – change us to make us fit for eternity. This is one reason why we have trial and trouble in our lives – it changes us. If we allow God to work it will change us for better but if we refuse to allow him to work then we may change for the worse. We can become bitter and angry or we can be softened and increase in our love for each other and our love for God. We have a choice.

A friend of mine was going through some bad times once and we were chatting about the way God works in our lives. "Well," she said, "I think my character has been changed enough now – I'd like to stay just as I am, thank you, and not have any more trials." I can understand that entirely and have often had similar thoughts myself. However, once we allow God into our lives he never gives up on us! Just as we would never give up on our own children, so he will continue his work with us and I know that at the end of my time here on earth I will thank him for that even if I sometimes forget to thank him now.

So I thank God that I am not just an automaton with no ability to think for myself or act for myself and because of that I am able to have a meaningful relationship with him. Above all, I thank God that in his plans and purposes he has made it possible for me to know him while I am here on earth and then later, after death, to be with him for eternity.

A Block of Marble Shaped by God

A block of hardest marble stood
Before the sculptor; where he would
He smote with hand well skilled,
And thus with blow on blow fulfilled
The vision of his mind.
At first with chisel coarse, and stroke
Unspared, the corners off he broke,
And soon the form appeared;
But then with finer tools he wrought –
And finer yet – until he brought
The perfect image forth.
So with unerring skilfulness,
With cunning hand and sure,
'Tis as the *marble* groweth less,

The *likeness* groweth more.
So God divinely works with those
He in the eternal ages chose
To show His works of grace,
And thus with blow on blow to trace
The image of His Son.

(A J H Brown)

Chapter 11
SORROW AND SUFFERING

"Why does God allow suffering?"

"Now that is a very big question and lots of books have been written about it which you might like to read."

"But what do you think?"

"Well, I can only speak from personal experience and I would say there is always a reason for it even if we don't understand it. For example, I have learned far more about God and his love during the difficult times in my life than I have when everything is going well."

"That's weird – I wonder why that is?"

"It has something to do with being human I suppose. You do see the concept in nature too of course."

"How?"

"Have you ever seen a chrysalis during the process of it becoming a butterfly? There is a real struggle to emerge from the cocoon but I understand that this process is necessary in order to create the beauty of the butterfly. If you try and take a short cut through the process you get a very drab and bedraggled butterfly that won't live long."

"So you are saying that, in ways we don't understand, suffering and sorrow form our characters?"

"Yes I am saying that but I am not saying I understand it. I do know though that without suffering and sorrow in the world there would not also be compassion and sympathy and kindness and so on because there would be no need to show these characteristics."

"I suppose so but you would think there could be another way."

"That's often the problem for us – we often think we know best. Instead of accepting that God has created things the way he has, we are sure we could think of a better way! Remember though that if you consider you could think of a better way it has to be a complete plan. You can't just remove the things you dislike because you have to remember that they all have an impact on something else. You can't just remove suffering without thinking what would happen to other things as a result."

"I hadn't thought of that before but I'm sure there must be a way to eradicate sorrow and suffering."

"Yes there is a perfect way and God will do it one day. There will be a day when there is no more sorrow, or suffering, or sin, or death – everything will be perfect. I am looking forward to that day when I will be with Jesus for all eternity. Will you be there too?"

"If there is such a place then I hope so."

"Perhaps you should give the question some time and attention in case you miss the opportunity."

In most of our lives there is often trouble and sorrow. These can sometimes come without warning or they can approach steadily and go on for a long time. Most of us have a burden to bear which is peculiarly ours and often cannot even be expressed to those near and dear to us. It is not that God causes such circumstances – sometimes we cause them ourselves – but he does allow them.

Cause and effect
There are different kinds of sorrow and suffering. We can experience emotional or physical suffering ourselves or we can see those we love suffering which is also very difficult to bear. At such times I have experienced different effects on my relationship with God. As we saw in the previous chapter, it is possible to either become bitter or angry or to grow in our love and closeness to the Lord Jesus. It is he who is able to comfort and help in situations

when no one else is able to do so. I am often asked this question about suffering – why does God allow (sometimes the person even says cause) suffering?

There is such a difference between God causing something and God allowing something to happen. He has set up our world with moral laws and consequences and when sin occurs there is always a consequence. It is sin that causes these problems – not necessarily our own – but somewhere, somehow, sin is always at the root of the sorrow and distress we encounter. That subject is, in itself, another whole book and cannot be covered here in depth.

There is a consequence to every sin and God allows these consequences. Sometimes he steps in directly and removes the consequence but often, at least in my experience, he does not. Just as children sometimes have to learn from their mistakes, so do we. We must always remember that God has given us freedom to choose. We can choose to do right or we can choose to do wrong. He does not take that freedom away from us and he wants us to freely love him. He does not impose himself, although he does sometimes come in directly, and in his sovereignty, to save us from the results of our own foolishness. He cannot always do this though. If he did, we have already seen that it would mean we did not really have freewill and thus we could not freely love him. So we have freewill and humankind has not always used this wisely in the past. This has had an effect on our lives today. Similarly, we ourselves do not always use our freedom to choose in the best way and thus we create problems for ourselves and others.

However, God knew in advance that this would happen and when we place our lives in his hands he is able to use all these things for our blessing. I have not experienced much physical suffering, unlike many I know, but I have known emotional suffering. At such times I have experienced the presence of God in a way I have never known when everything is going well. Would I prefer not to have had such 'suffering'? Yes, of course I would. Would I prefer not to have had such suffering *if that was the only way I could deepen my relationship with God?* Now, that is quite a different question and I cannot think of anything which is more valuable to me than my knowledge of God and my relationship with him through the Lord Jesus Christ. I do therefore thank him for those difficult times because I know him better as a result. Did I thank him at the time?

No I did not, I just tried to rely on his love. It is often only later in our lives when we look back at the things we have gone through that we are able to thank God for them.

I find that when things are not going well I spend more time in prayer and conversation with God. Just as we grow more like the people we spend time with and begin to understand them better, so it is with God. Things I did not understand once, I do understand now and I am sure that things I do not understand now I may well understand at some time in the future. As my relationship deepens with him so I should become more acquainted with the way he speaks with me and I learn how to listen.

Comfort in distress

God has often spoken to me very clearly when I have been distressed and these are some of the things he has said to me:

'Never will I leave you; never will I forsake you (Hebrews 13:5).'
'I am with you and will watch over you wherever you go (Genesis 28:15).'
'Be strong and courageous. Do not be afraid; do not be discouraged (Joshua 1:9),'
'For I know the plans I have for you, plans to prosper you and not to harm you, plans to give you hope and a future (Jeremiah 29:11).'
'…no-one who has left home or brothers or sisters or mother or father or children or fields for me and the gospel will fail to receive a hundred times as much……….(Mark 10:28-30)'
'Come to me, all you who are weary and burdened, and I will give you rest (Matthew 11:28).'

You will realize that these words God has spoken to me come from the Bible. Yes, of course they do. Why would God not use his Word to speak to me and comfort me. He often does. Not always of course, but often he does and this means that I can be sure it is God speaking. The Bible is invaluable to me because if I check what I hear with the Bible and find it there I can be sure that it is God who is speaking.

I have often had the experience of hearing God speaking to me and not being sure if it was his voice. I have turned to the Bible and found the words or phrase somewhere there when I did not know such a verse or phrase ever existed. Yes, sometimes I know it is from the Bible and obviously more so now because I know my Bible better than I did. However, I still often find in my prayers or conversations with God that a verse will come to me quite clearly and it is as if I never knew it before -   absolutely right for the moment, comforting, encouraging, guiding or whatever else I might need. I have certainly discovered the truth that the Bible is a living word which is 'sharper than any double-edged sword'. In Hebrews 4:12 we read:- 'For the word of God is alive and active. Sharper than any double-edged sword, it penetrates even to dividing soul and spirit, joints and marrow; it judges the thoughts and attitudes of the heart.'

Why me?

I sometimes hear people say, 'why me?' when things go wrong. I don't often hear them say, 'why not me?' but that is an equally good question. We are all part of a broken world which has been spoiled by sin and we are all affected by that at certain times in our lives. I also hear people say that it's 'not fair' – and of course it's not fair! Man has made wrong choices from the beginning of time which means that life is not fair.

Adam began by choosing to do wrong and disobeying God which was the first step towards the problems which have subsequently arisen. However, the worst example of 'unfairness' is surely seen in the cross of the Lord Jesus Christ. Jesus had never done anything wrong and his accusers could find nothing to justify his crucifixion. Even Pilate said he could find no fault with him. So Pilate gave the people the choice – choose Jesus or Barabbas; choose good or evil; choose for life to be fair or to be unfair! No wonder life is not fair, why should it be when we have made such disastrous choices?

We have already seen that there are always consequences to our actions and our choices and these do not just affect us – sometimes they affect future generations. You might be thinking that had you been there when Jesus was arrested you would not have made such a choice. That's good because today you have the chance to reverse the judgement of the world on Jesus. You can accept him as your Lord and Saviour and thank him for all that he has suffered on your account. He is and was God and he had the power then to simply return to heaven rather than die on a cross. He chose not to do so because of his love for me – and for you. You may not have clamoured for his death on that day, but you have done and said other things that are wrong. Just as he said on that day, 'Father forgive them,' so he will also forgive you. The Bible says that, 'Everyone who calls on the name of the Lord will be saved.'(Romans 10:13) And that includes me and it includes you.

So does this mean that life will then become fair? No, I am afraid it does not because we are part of a broken world and life will continue to be unfair because of all that has gone before. Whether you know God or whether you don't you are still part of that world and as a result have to suffer the consequences of sin. However, this will not always be the case. The good news for each of us is that although life sometimes seems unfair, God *is* fair and just and righteous and perfect. There is a day coming when all the injustice and unfairness of life will be corrected. I have given my life to Jesus and I know that, as a result, God will work through all the unfairness and use everything for my blessing. God has given me this promise:- '….in all things God works for the good of those who love him……' (Romans 8:28) So whether the things that happen to me are fair or unfair I know that God will use them all for my eventual benefit.

From suffering to glory

The Bible also says, 'I consider that our present sufferings are not worth comparing with the glory that will be revealed in us.' (Romans 8:18) Whether I am a Christian or not I will, at some time in my life, have sorrow or suffering. However, if I give my life to God and allow him to work in me and through me he will use *everything* to make me fit for my life with him eternally. So I believe that there is a day coming when life will be fair and it will be perfect and when that day comes God will explain anything I want to know about what happened while I was here on earth. In the meantime I am content to trust him. He has already shown me how much he loves me because the Lord Jesus died on the cross for me. That being the case I can trust his love and know that everything will work out for my good even if I don't understand it all now.

I referred earlier in this chapter to the process of nature at work when a butterfly emerges and the necessity of the struggle that ensues. The following piece is a beautiful example of why God sometimes allows suffering in our lives.

Perfect through suffering

I kept, for nearly a year, the flasked-shaped cocoon of an Emperor moth. It is very peculiar in its construction. A narrow opening is left in the neck of the flask, through which the perfect insect forces its way, so that a forsaken cocoon is as entire as one still tenanted, no rupture of the interlacing fibres having taken place.

The great disproportion between the means of egress and the size of the prisoned insect makes one wonder how the exit is ever accomplished at all, and it never is without great labour and difficulty. It is supposed that the pressure to which the moth's body is subjected in passing through the narrow opening is a provision of nature for forcing the juices into vessels of the wings, these being less developed at the period of emergence from the chrysalis than they are in other insects.

I happened to witness the first efforts of my imprisoned moth to escape from its long confinement. Nearly a whole morning, from time to time, I watched it patiently striving and struggling to get out. It never seemed able to get beyond a certain point, and at last my patience was exhausted. I thought I was wiser and more compassionate than its Maker and resolved to give it a helping hand.

With the points of my scissors I snipped the confining threads to make the exit just a very little easier, and I was so pleased to see that immediately, and with perfect ease out crawled the body. But my pleasure was short-lived as I saw with horror that it was a swollen body and little shrivelled wings! In vain I watched to see that marvellous progress of expansion in which the wings silently and swiftly develop before our eyes, and as I traced the exquisite spots and working of diverse colours which were all there in miniature, I longed to see these assume their due proportions, and the creature appear in all its perfect beauty, as it is one of the loveliest of its kind.

But I looked in vain; my false tenderness had proved its ruin. It never was anything but a stunted abortion, crawling painfully through that brief life which it should have spent flying through the air on rainbow wings.

The lesson I got that day has often stood me in good stead. It has helped me to understand what is sometimes called 'the hardness of God's love'. I have thought of it often when watching with pitiful eyes those who were struggling with sorrows, suffering or distress, and it has seemed to me that I was more merciful than God and I would have given deliverance. Short-sighted fool! How could I know that even one of those pains and groans could be spared? The far-sighted, perfect love of God, which seeks the perfection of its object, does not weakly shrink from present transient suffering. Our Father's love is too true to be weak. Because he loves His children He chastens them, that they may 'share in His holiness'. With this glorious end in view, he does not spare their crying. We are made perfect through suffering – our example is Christ himself – and we are trained in obedience and finally brought to glory.

(Author unknown)

Chapter 12
COMMITMENT

"You have been talking about sorrow and hard times and so on but are you never afraid that perhaps God isn't there, or perhaps he is too busy to listen to you or something?"

"Yes I have had that experience of calling out to the Lord and feeling that he is just not hearing me."

"That must have been awful for you."

"Yes and I think perhaps that when that has happened it is worse than the actual circumstances I am going through. I have felt I could cope with the sorrow but the anguish of thinking I am not heard by God is much worse than the sorrow of the moment."

"So why wouldn't God answer you directly at such a time?"

"I don't know the full answer to that but I do know that I have learned a lot even through that."

"Like what then?"

"It was during such a time that I found the comfort and the beauty of the Psalms in the Bible."

"Really? Why was that then?"

"Well, there is so much emotion in the Psalms. I can see the anguish and distress felt by those long ago and it mirrors what I may feel today. I can see how their sorrow turns to joy and this is a real encouragement. It makes me feel I am not alone in how I feel but my emotions are similar to those of others who knew God."

"Sounds interesting."

"Yes it certainly is. Most of all it shows me how God is so faithful and never let those people down. Although they had sorrow, they also had much joy and I find the same in my own life. There is far too much to try and describe here and really the only way you will understand is if you read the Psalms for yourself."

"Yes maybe I should."

Yes there have been times in my relationship with God when I speak and there is no answer. Perhaps I should say there appears to be no answer. The anguish and the grief of calling out to the Lord and there seems to be nothing except a blanket of silence. I have had those times – awful times – during my journey with God. For several years now though I thank God this has not been the case – but such a time may come again. If it does I will try to remember all the lessons learned during the past, but of course I may not!

Why not?

So why is this? Why should there be no reply – or appear to be no reply. If God loves me, as I know he does, and if he wants to have a relationship with me, as I know he does, why this apparent silence? The reasons are many and varied and I can only speak of those I know.

Firstly it could be that I am living or acting in a wrong way and my sin has separated me from him. In the Old Testament the Israelites had turned away from God and the prophet Isaiah had to say to them, 'Surely the arm of the Lord is not too short to save, nor his ear too dull to hear. But your iniquities have separated you from your God; your sins have hidden his face from you, so that he will not hear' (Isaiah 59:1-2). We cannot expect to behave in any way we please yet still expect to be in a close relationship with God.

Or perhaps it might be carelessness rather than wrongdoing. It could be that I have left God and carried on with my life as if he were not there. Left him from my thoughts and my conversations. Left him in the way I am living. Yes, I have done all this. As we have already seen, sometimes when everything in life is running smoothly it is easy to take it all for granted and never give a thought to the One who has made it all possible. The Bible says that, 'In his hand is the life of every creature and the breath of all mankind (Job

12:10).' Whether we recognize it or not, God is able to determine the time of our birth and our death. Our life is literally in his hands and if he decides to step in at any moment then he is able to do so. Nevertheless, in our foolishness or in our pride, we forget this and live our lives as if nothing matters more than our own enjoyment.

Perhaps there is an even bigger danger for those who are 'religious'. How easy it is – I know – to do all the right things and say all the right things (at least on the surface) and yet be far away from God – perhaps not even knowing that it is possible to have a close and personal relationship with him. How sad that the Bible tells us there will be a day when the Lord will have to say to some that he does not know them:- '....you begin to stand outside and knock at the door, saying 'Lord, Lord, open for us,' and he will answer and say to you 'I do not know you,........(Luke 13:25 NKJV).' A solemn warning to those who cling to their religions but never personally know the Lord Jesus for themselves.

A way back

So there is also the silence that comes from never having known God – I never knew you – it was all in your imagination. There is the silence that comes from having known God and been close to him and then departing from him. I can turn away in anger, in grief, in selfishness, in carelessness and in other ways too. If I choose to go my own way, if I never consult him about my plans, if I do things that I know will not meet with his approval, can I really expect an immediate and clear reply when I do decide to speak to him?

Now having said that, if I recognize where I have gone wrong, or are going wrong; if I am calling to him because I realize that somewhere somehow I have left him; then I am certain there will be a response. The difficulty is that I so often speak to him with a hidden agenda. I want him to change my circumstances perhaps. I want to avoid the consequences of my own foolish decisions. I am perhaps even angry with God because things are not going my way. Having made my decisions and my plans – without consulting him – I now find myself in trouble and want God to step in and change things.

But there are also those times when I just do not know why I feel that God is not there. In Isaiah 45:15 the Bible says, 'Truly you are a God who has been hiding himself,' and there may be times that God does hide himself and we do not know why. God is God and has a right to do as he pleases, so there will be times when I simply do not understand. However, I do know that I can still rely on his love – irrespective of how I feel – because as we saw in the last chapter he has promised never to leave me. So I must trust in his love and faithfulness and not on my feelings. It was an important step forward in my relationship with God when I began to realize that I should learn to rely on *his* promises and not on *my* feelings.

And so I have called out to God and had no apparent answer. In sin, in selfishness, in carelessness or in anger I may have turned away. However, the marvellous wonder of God is that there is always a way back to him! You will have noticed already that when I speak of a lack of response from God I hope I have been careful to always say an *apparent* lack of response. The truth is that God always hears us and will always answer us – but not always immediately and certainly not always with a yes! God may say yes, he may say no, or he may say wait and often it is not even clear he is saying anything at all. But faith says – and as you journey with God experience begins to say too – that he will answer in the right way and at the right time.

His way not mine

Just because I don't hear or experience an immediate response does not mean that God is not speaking. Most of the time if I don't hear it is because of my own state and especially my own will getting in the way. For many years I thought God was ignoring me. All I asked for seemed to be refused. I had a perfect plan, so I thought, for myself but God was just not playing ball! It never occurred to me to just say – with an open mind – Lord what is *your* will for my life! I didn't think it would mean emotional distance from my family – but it has. I didn't think it would mean not getting married until I was 41 – but it did. I didn't think it would mean not having any children – but it did. I certainly didn't think it meant joining the Church of England! I had a horror of that church and thought it was the epitome of everything that was wrong about Christianity and religion but I had a hard lesson to learn – that actually it was I who was the epitome of everything that was wrong! Yes this particular Christian denomination has its faults, as has every

Christian denomination, but it also includes some of the most wonderful people I have ever met who are demonstrating God's wonderful love to others. Of course you may say that this is true of every group of Christians and you may well be right. I know many groups where this is so and I don't know them all so I can only speak of what I know. That is not the point I am trying to make however. The point I wish to make is that God had to teach me a very hard lesson because of my preconceived opinions about a group of people I had never met. The point I am trying to make is, that if there appears to be no response from God, then maybe I should consider whether it may be my fault rather than his!

Do you have a purpose?

So why then does God sometimes say 'wait' and not answer immediately when I ask for things? Did you know that God is more concerned with the sort of person you are rather than the things you do. Our life here is to form our character to be more like Jesus and thus be fit for an eternity with him. What is the purpose of your life? Do you even have one? What will people be able to say about you after you have gone? Most important of all, what will God say about you?

When you meet with God at the end of time will he have to say to you that you entirely missed the whole purpose of ever having been alive on earth? The whole purpose of our living is so that we can come into relationship with God, so that he can work with us and form us so that we are ready to spend eternity with him. So in the waiting and the disappointments and everything else in my life I can say that God is working out his plan and purpose for me. Sometimes I understand what he is doing, often I do not, but I do know his love and can trust in that.

I have spoken of my turning away but the wonderful thing about a relationship with God is that he never does. The Bible tells us that if we are unfaithful, he remains faithful. With earthly relationships we can never be one hundred percent sure that the other person will always remain faithful. Whether it be family or friends, so often problems arise which are never resolved even if we try hard from our side to make it right. With God this is never the case. He is always willing to resume the relationship where we left off. He is always with me – even if I leave him. He is always ready to forgive when I turn back to him and he is always working in my life to make sure that the end result is just as he wishes it to be!

So when we talk about the commitment in a relationship, we know it takes two people to commit and two people to be faithful. There is always a danger that one or the other will renege. The behaviour of one or the other – or both – might mean the relationship is destroyed for ever. With God it is completely different. Once we have entered into a relationship with him then it is for ever. Nothing we can do or say will make him unfaithful or make him leave us. It is a commitment not just for this life but also for eternity! Why would you not want a relationship like that!

The Psalms

I did not always have this conviction though. I remember specifically a time when I was in much distress – and this was after I had begun my relationship with God. I could not understand why I was going through this dark time in my life and why God was allowing it all to happen. I began to doubt God and I thought that if I was really a Christian and had a real relationship with God then this would not be happening. I would not be depressed like this and in such anguish. I went to bed that night very down and more by habit than intention I briefly picked up my Bible. Feeling too dispirited to read I was about to put it down again when I realized I had opened it at the Psalms. I read Psalm 13 - 'How long O Lord? Will you forget me for ever? How long will you hide your face from me? How long must I wrestle with my thoughts and every day have sorrow in my heart?' - and the most incredible peace filled my heart. Even David, that hero of the Bible, one who without doubt knew God, had these times of deep distress and anguish. Did it mean that his relationship with God was in doubt? No, of course not! Did it mean that God had turned away? No, of course not! Did it mean that his relationship with God could never again reach the wonderful heights that it had before? No of course not! The many and varied Psalms illustrate the terrific highs and lows that we do experience in a relationship with God. Perhaps I should say that *I* experience because I cannot speak for you. But oh the joy and peace that came from knowing that I was not alone! Here I was in the company of

David and other men of God experiencing similar emotions and God working through it all to perfect his work in me!

I was so glad to read the Psalms that night and went to bed with my load lifted. I wonder why I happened to chance upon them just at that time – what a coincidence!

Wait

Desperately, helplessly, longingly, I cried:
Quietly, patiently, lovingly God replied.

I pled and I wept for a clue to my fate,
And the Master so gently said, "Child, you must wait".

"Wait? You say, wait!" my indignant reply.
"Lord, I need answers, I need to know why!
Is your hand shortened? Or have you not heard?
By Faith, I have asked, and am claiming your Word.
My future and all to which I can relate
hangs in the balance, and YOU tell me to WAIT?
I'm needing a 'yes', a go-ahead sign,
or even a 'no' to which I can resign.
And Lord, You promised that if we believe
we need but to ask, and we shall receive.
And Lord, I've been asking, and this is my cry:
I'm weary of asking! I need a reply!

Then quietly, softly, I learned of my fate
As my Master replied once again, "You must wait."

So, I slumped in my chair, defeated and taut
and grumbled to God, "So, I'm waiting.... for what?"

He seemed, then, to kneel, and His eyes wept with mine,
And He tenderly said, "I could give you a sign.
I could shake the heavens, and darken the sun.
I could raise the dead, and cause mountains to run.
All you seek, I could give, and pleased you would be.
You would have what you want--But, you wouldn't know Me.

You'd not know the depth of My love for each saint;
You'd not know the power that I give to the faint;
You'd not learn to see through the clouds of despair;
You'd not learn to trust just by knowing I'm there;
You'd not know the joy of resting in Me
When darkness and silence were all you could see.

You'd never experience that fullness of love
As the peace of My Spirit descends like a dove;
You'd know that I give and I save.... (for a start),
But you'd not know the depth of the beat of My heart.

The glow of My comfort late into the night,
The faith that I give when you walk without sight,
The depth that's beyond getting just what you asked
Of an infinite God, who makes what you have LAST.

You'd never know, should your pain quickly flee,
What it means that "My grace is sufficient for Thee."
Yes, your dreams for your loved one overnight would come true,
But, Oh, the loss! If I lost what I'm doing in you!

So, be silent, my child, and in time you will see
That the greatest of gifts is to get to know Me.
And though oft' may My answers seem terribly late,
My most precious answer of all is still, "WAIT."

(Author unknown)

Chapter 13
CHALLENGES

"Did you see that report the other day about all those people who are starving overseas? All those people suffering?"

"Yes of course I did. It is a terrible thing to see people suffering."

"So why is it happening?"

"What are you doing about it?"

"Me? What's it got to do with me? I only asked you why it is happening? You say God loves us and all that but it doesn't seem much like love to me when I see those reports."

"What are you doing about it?"

"You have already said that and I don't see it has anything to do with me."

"Aren't you saddened and horrified by all those people suffering?"

"Yes of course I am but what can I do about it?"

"Quite a lot actually!"

"Me? I am just one person and I can't solve that sort of problem. These sorts of problems should be God's responsibility – after all, he is all-powerful."

"You mean, pass the buck to him so you don't have to actually do anything?"

"Well, I can't go there and lend a hand can I? I have responsibilities here where I live."

"Yes that's right and I'm not suggesting you go anywhere just now. Do you have enough to live on?"

"Yes nearly I suppose. I could do with a really good holiday and my car is getting a bit old now but we're not too badly off."

"I wonder when those starving people last had a holiday."

"Oh yes that's right we were talking about them weren't we. I forgot all about them for a moment when I started thinking about my next holiday."

"Ah I see."

"Oh dear, I think I can see what you are getting at now! I did put a tenner in the collection tin for them the other day – will that help?"

"Yes of course it will – at least that's a start. If everyone did that then that would at least be a start towards solving the problems there are of deprivation all over the world."

"Do you mean that some of these problems are my fault and not God's as I sometimes think?"

"Well not you personally exactly but selfishness and greed are the main contributors. If you contribute towards the selfishness and greed then yes that does make you partly responsible. Did you know that there is actually enough food, water and other necessities in the world to ensure that no one goes without?"

"I had heard something like that but never taken much notice. Oh dear, I sort of wish I had never started this conversation."

"Well a lot of people do blame God you know for these problems but they don't usually bother to speak to him about them."

"I think I can see why! I did ask him why it was all happening and now you have said this I am getting a bit uncomfortable about it all. There is a lot more I could do without it affecting my standard of

living that much and, of course, even more I could do if I was prepared to sometimes go without something for myself."

"I'll leave you to think about it all then shall I?"

"If I gave a bit more regularly would that help? But I wonder where it would be best to pay it – you hear about all the corruption there is in different charities and money not getting through to the right place and so on."

"Yes I hear that excuse used a lot for the reason why people won't give. It's quite convenient really isn't it!"

"I suppose it is. But it is difficult to know the best way to give."

"The only difficult thing is making a start! If you speak to God about it and then make a start you may be surprised at what happens next. In any case you will be pleasing God in what you are doing and he will then guide you and direct you in the details."

Sometimes my relationship with God is very challenging. I can be going along quite comfortably and then suddenly I can be stopped in my tracks. Certain questions come into my mind and begin to make me feel quite uncomfortable. We have seen in the last chapter that often the question is asked: 'why does God allow suffering?' As we have seen that is a big question and many books have been written specifically on the subject. There are many reasons why God allows suffering but the challenge for me here was very personal.

Avoiding the issue

For many years I never really thought much about all the suffering there was in the world. I found it uncomfortable to see the images of starving children, on the news or in the paper. My solution was to skip over it and not pay too much attention. It never occurred to me that actually I could help to do something about it!

Then one day God spoke to me clearly from the Bible. I was reading in the book of James (you will find this in the New

Testament) and not paying too much attention perhaps because I was rather tired at the time. Suddenly and without warning the words jumped out at me: 'What good is it Margaret, if you claim to have faith but have no deeds' (James 2:14). Help! I stopped and read it again. Of course, it didn't actually say Margaret on the page but as far as I was concerned it might as well have done so, such was the impact on me. I read it again and then continued to read on and tried to forget it. I put the Bible down but still the verse went round in my head. So, I opened the Bible again and read the whole section around that particular sentence. Suddenly I realized that, here I was, a human being, a Christian even, doing absolutely nothing about certain situations when I had the means to do so!

I knew of course that this had nothing to do with my salvation and my faith. I was clear, and still am, that my salvation and my eternal destiny are totally on the basis of faith. My works, however good or however bad, do not affect the fact that I am saved, and safe, because Jesus died for me and shed his precious blood for me. I cannot add to that or take away from that by any 'deeds' of my own. Suddenly it was being brought home to me, in no uncertain terms, that this very fact had blinded me to the truth that there was something I should be doing! I was taking God's love for granted. Did I realize how much love had been shown to me? Obviously not nearly enough or surely I would have been anxious to show that love to others.

I also know that we will never have a perfect world until the Lord Jesus returns at his second coming. I realize now that I used this as an excuse – 'oh things will always be like this until the Lord comes' I would say carelessly. In other words, I don't have to make any effort now and can sit back and enjoy all the blessings I have without having to make any changes in my life now. Even better, if I simply start talking about what a wonderful day that will be then it means I don't have to do anything now! What hypocrisy and religion at its worst. Say all the right things and use all the right words and do absolutely nothing!

What can I do?

What an uncomfortable lesson this was to start to learn. I am sure I still have much more to learn too! However, it was the beginning of a change of attitude and a question, 'Lord, what do you want me to do?'

There was no voice from the sky, no flashing lights and for the moment only silence but having asked the question I was again at peace. I knew that, if there was something for me to do then it would be made clear – and it was and it is. At the moment not much I know, but I want to try to be faithful in the little things God has given me to do and always be ready if there should be anything else.

I have to confess that I have always been full of admiration but also a little envious of those Christians who are doing so much good. Those who have youth clubs in the inner cities, those who work overseas in the trouble spots of the world, those who start up shelters for the homeless and many, many more wonderful things. They are filled with the love of God for others and are willing to give up their comforts, their time, their money and much more besides because they want to show this love to others. I aspire to be like them whilst at the same time recognising my own weakness.

However, at the same time, I need to make sure that I do what God wants me to do. This may be small or it may be great but it will be exactly the right job for me, if it is in God's plan for me. I believe God spoke to me about this particular matter one day when I was at a concert. The orchestra was playing and I was enjoying the music when my attention was suddenly attracted to the player with the triangle. There he stood, near the back, nearly hidden from those around him and holding only a triangle. Standing there motionless as the music played, I thought, 'what use is he?' Then as the music continued, suddenly he became more alert; I could almost see his hands trembling with anticipation! There it came, the sweet sudden sound of a few notes on the triangle. Adding to the wonderful sound, exactly in the right place and at the right time it made its contribution to the overall sound and perfection of this particular piece of music. I didn't see if he played again – I don't think he did – but I spent the rest of the concert thinking about this. The image is obvious I think. If we work together under the guidance and direction of the Great Conductor then everything will happen at the right time and in the right place. Whether it be the first violins or the great bass drum or the tiny triangle, all are necessary if the right sound is to be made. Whether my part is small or great, let me do it with all my might and do it right! What a muddle if the triangle player suddenly decides to take over the drum! Who would play the triangle then and the drummer, not knowing how to play a triangle, would find himself redundant. In God's kingdom there is a place for everyone and a part for everyone to play under his guidance and care.

Something for me to do

Because I like to be specific when I can, I want to tell you some small but specific things this challenge led me to do. Prior to God speaking to me through James, I had heard that it was possible to sponsor a child overseas. You may know this already, but at that time, I had only recently heard about it – and had ignored it. That sort of information usually went right over my head. I was not deliberately ignoring it; it was more that I just didn't think it applied to me. It applied to other people perhaps, but not me. When I had occasionally thought a bit more about such things I just decided that the problems in the world were just too big for me to do anything about and this was one further example.

When God spoke to me however I was prompted to look into this idea a bit more. I had some idea it was an organization called Tearfund that was involved so I looked at their website but didn't find the information about sponsoring a child. However, I did find lots of other information which really grabbed my attention and as a result I began a relationship with that organization which continues to this day. In fact, I am now the Tearfund representative for our church and am becoming increasingly passionate about the work this organization does – what a coincidence that I looked at their website!

At a later date I did find the information about sponsoring a child overseas for a better future and so I also began a relationship with that organization (CompassionUK), and sponsored a child in Uganda, which continues to this day. So instead of being able to help and influence one child through sponsorship I am also helping others in suffering and need in different parts of the world through my connection with Tearfund. God has his own ways of getting us involved where he wants us to be.

I explain all this only to give a practical example of how God often works in my life. You might think that what I do is not much – and I must admit I am tempted to think that too. On the other hand, I believe I am doing what God wants me to do in this particular area of my life. It might not be much but if everyone who has more than they need was prepared to sponsor one child or give a small amount monthly to such organizations as those mentioned then the world's problems would be drastically reduced – maybe even eliminated! There is enough food and water in the world to meet the needs of every individual. The problem is the way man uses what is there and how, or if, he distributes it wisely. Many of us take too much and as a result many do not have enough.

Anybody or Nobody?

I believe that God has spoken to me very clearly about these matters of suffering and my involvement. How easy it is to blame God when things are wrong instead of asking myself if there is anything I can do. If I do think about it at all then perhaps I think that someone else will do what is necessary. Perhaps my neighbour or a charity or even the church. I used to have a saying on the wall of my office which went something like this: -

'There were once four people named Everybody, Somebody, Anybody and Nobody. There was an important job to be done and Everybody was sure that Somebody would do it. Anybody could have done it, but Nobody did it. Somebody got upset about that, because it was Everybody's job. Everybody thought Anybody could do it, but Nobody realized that Everybody wouldn't do it. It ended up that Everybody blamed Somebody when Nobody did what Anybody could have done.'

I was good at applying this in my office but when it came to the problem of suffering in the world – well, somebody would do it!

It is because of the greed and selfishness of man that many of these problems have arisen. We, in the West, who have plenty, often do not pay a fair price for goods from poorer countries. We want more and more and we often don't care, or even think about, the cost factor for others who are supplying the goods. We have the knowledge and the money to solve some of the problems caused by climate changes in other parts of the world but we do nothing. Instead, we continue to wallow in our self-indulgent life-styles and if we do ever think about these issues we salve our conscience by blaming God! One day God will indeed step in and right the wrongs but in the meantime, I ask myself, what are you doing about it?

Relationships are not always easy and when God challenges me it is not comfortable but it *is* necessary.

Only One

I am only one,
But still I am one.
I cannot do everything,
But still I can do something;
And because I cannot do
Everything
I will not refuse to do the
Something that I can do.

(Edward Everett Hale)

Chapter 14
CHURCH FAMILY

"Why do you go to church?"

"Because I want to learn more about God."

"Do you enjoy going?"

"Yes most of the time I do."

"Well the times when I have been I have found it incredibly boring."

"That might say more about you than it says about the church though! However, I am sure that some services are boring, so it might not just be you. It depends on whether the Holy Spirit is present and active there and it also depends on you to some extent."

"What do you mean about the Holy Spirit bit?"

"Do you remember we were discussing the Holy Spirit earlier? If I know and love Jesus then God will give me the gift of the Holy Spirit who then lives in me with my spirit. However, you will remember that I can either give him plenty of room to operate or I can just carry on as if he is not there."

"Yes I do remember that. He is gentle and won't push into situations if I don't want him there. Ah, so that's what you must mean about the church. If the people there are allowing him space to operate then God will be speaking and it won't be boring."

"Yes, that's right – but remember I also said it depends on you – and me, to some extent."

"Why is that then?"

"Why did you go to church when you went."

"Oh I think it was a wedding or Christmas or something like that."

"And did you expect to hear from God?"

"No of course I didn't!"

"Well you got exactly what you expected then! The trouble is that often I go to church with no expectation of hearing from God so I don't really listen out for him. Or perhaps I always go to get something and never think of taking anything myself."

"What's that supposed to mean? I didn't know you had to take things when you went to church!"

"Well I often go just because I want to thank and praise God for all the wonderful things he has done for me so I am taking my thanks. I also sometimes go because I want to meet up with other Christians I know to see how they are getting on in their journey with God. So I suppose you could say I am taking a concern for others with me."

"I had never thought of that before. I thought you went to church to get something for yourself."

"That is usually my experience – that I do get some wonderful new understanding of God, or some guidance about things in my life, or some particular word of comfort or love if I am in a difficult situation. However, if we only ever go because we want to get and never think of taking anything, then that will be another reason why the church service might seem a bit dry at times. If everyone wants to get and no one wants to give then the atmosphere will be a bit selfish won't it!"

"Yes I suppose it will but if I came along, I wouldn't feel I had much to give."

"Don't worry about that because I have often been like that and there have always been some wonderful people there who have obviously come to give and so I have received plenty. Also, thankfully God often gives irrespective of our self-centredness so we can rely on him and not on ourselves. We should think about these things though because for one thing it stops us being so critical about everyone else!"

"I do understand that. It is easy to just criticize everyone else without really thinking whether I could do any better. I suppose if we looked for the best in each person and loved them the way you say God loves us then church would be a much better experience for everyone."

"I couldn't have put it better myself."

I love going to church! Yes I'm sorry if that sounds ridiculous to you but I actually enjoy going to church. God often speaks to me there, I meet some of the most wonderful people anyone could wish to meet and I sometimes have experiences there that I have never had anywhere else. However, I could not always have said that of my 'church' experiences.

Experiences of church

I have had many and varied experiences of church. I used to go to Christian meetings which were not in a church and now I go to a building which is a church for Christian meetings or services. However, did you know that the word 'church' in the Bible does not refer to a building of bricks and stone at all. The original Greek word was 'ekklesia' which means an assembly or gathering of people and we have gradually changed this word in our thinking so that many people today think that 'church' just means a building.

In the Bible we are told that the 'church' on earth is a living building made up of all God's people. So, everyone who knows God and loves the Lord Jesus is part of this building irrespective of whether they have ever been in a church building. God knows each one. The church in the Bible is also likened to the body of the Lord Jesus here on earth. Each of us that know him represent him in some way and together we form his body on earth. This is why Christians usually love to meet up together, whether this is in a church building, a house, or some other building. It does not matter what denomination I belong to because if I belong to Christ I am part of his body here on earth. How dangerous it is therefore for one or other Christian denominations to think that they are somehow better or have more truth than another. Only God knows that and he is not pleased if you are judging or condemning another denomination where there will be people who love him. He is interested in whether you personally know him through the Lord Jesus Christ and whether you personally are trying to live your life to please him. He will then guide you as to where you should go and with whom you should meet to learn more about him and to do his work on earth. However, you have to have an open mind to hear him when he directs you and not be like me who thought I already knew where he wanted me to be, so for a long time I actually never bothered to ask him!

It is a wonderful thing to have the assurance of being called by God and being in the place where he wants you to be. It is then that my relationship with God is able to really progress. I don't go to church because I have to or because anyone thinks I should or because there will be a big fuss if I don't go. I go because I really want to go; I go because I want to deepen my relationship with God; I go because I want to thank and praise God with others who feel the same; I go because I believe it pleases God when I do and I go because I love him. At the same time, I must always be aware that there may be a time when God wants me to do something for him, or learn something from him, elsewhere. I pray that I will never get so comfortable that I once again cease to hear him when he is trying to get my attention. God can move us out of our comfort zone from time to time but it is always with our blessing in mind.

A critical attitude

So as you can probably see I have had many experiences of church. Yes I have been bored sometimes but, in my case, looking back I can see that was my fault and not the fault of the church. One of the biggest problems that we can take with us into church is a critical attitude. It will always hinder us from hearing God speaking to us and from enjoying our experience there. I have often been very critical of others, in church, who don't behave as I think they should without giving a thought as to my own behaviour. There is a lovely illustration of this in the Bible about criticising others over small things and missing my own shortcomings entirely. God has had to speak to me clearly about this many times. 'Why do you look at the speck of sawdust in your brother's eye and pay no attention to the plank in your own eye? How can you say to your brother, "let me take the speck out of your eye" when all the time there is a plank in your own eye? You hypocrite, first take the plank out of your own eye and then you will see clearly to remove the speck from your brother's eye' (Matthew 7:3-5). As we have already seen, my relationship with God is not always comfortable, but then that is because it is a *real* relationship.

Worship

Do I have to go to church (and I am using church in the correct sense here – a gathering of Christians) in order to learn about God and in order to thank and praise him? No of course not. I can, and do, learn about him when I am alone. I can, and do, praise and worship him when I am alone. However, I have had some very special experiences when I have been with others who love God. I believe I have heard God speak to me very clearly, especially during times of praise and worship. There can be some very powerful lessons learned and some wonderful experiences of worship to be had when together with others who love Jesus. This has been my personal experience.

But you may be wondering what I mean when I talk about worship. The word is not often used in our everyday language and sometimes we can forget what it really means. The word worship really means that I am totally focused on someone or something to the exclusion of everything else. Many definitions link the word worship with God or a deity but it can apply elsewhere. We hear of some men 'worshipping' their wives; we hear, sadly, of people 'worshipping' a pop idol or a football team. If I focus exclusively on something then maybe I am 'worshipping' that thing. This is why the Bible tells us to worship only God. He is the only One who deserves our total attention and he is the One we should worship and put first in our lives.

I get the chance to focus exclusively on God in church when I may find it difficult in the everyday business of life. Yes I can, and do, find time alone with God which can at times also be very special but I also find I experience some amazing times with God when I am in church, i.e. with others who also love him. I have said that I want to know more about God and to deepen my relationship with him. It follows therefore that I would want to do anything that might help me in this – including meeting with others who know God, or in other words, 'going to church'. I have already covered the subject of God speaking to me through other people and here, in church, I have many opportunities to learn more about God from others who also know him.

I have learned so much from other people in Alpha groups, Ladies Group and so on. I have also learned so much from the wonderful people at my church. I could list name after name here of people who have helped me tremendously and often they have been completely unaware of it. People who have, in some way, shown me God's love in the things they have said and the words they have spoken. I thank God for guiding me in the way he has. You may remember in an earlier chapter I said that if God had answered all my prayers in the way I wanted him to then I would not have met many of the wonderful people I have met. Many of them are here at this church – and once upon a time I was afraid to even enter a church building! I know my experience of meeting such people is not unique and many people throughout the world could tell you the same thing. This is a further reason why it is so important to meet with others who love God – we can learn so much from them. Whether it be in a church building, a meeting hall, a café, a school, a small group in a home or wherever it is, if you meet together with people who know and love the Lord Jesus then I am sure God will use this to deepen your relationship with him.

I have had to learn that God knows best. He knows the best place for me and the best people to put around me so that I can deepen in my knowledge of him and in my relationship with him. Thank God it all depends on him and not on me or where would I be now! I dread to think where my cherished plans may have landed me and once again can thank him that he does not always say yes to my prayer requests!

If you are curious about church then why not try a visit? First though, speak to God about it and ask him to direct you to the best place for you to go. You may not hear a voice from the sky, I didn't, but he will hear you and he will direct you even if you are not immediately aware of it. If he did it for me then he will do it for you because he loves me and he also loves you.

If you don't understand anything about worship then don't worry about that. These things don't usually happen overnight but when you begin a relationship with God by asking Jesus into your life then you are on the road towards worship. One day you will probably find you are suddenly overwhelmed by the goodness and the love of God and all that he has done for you and you will be able to do nothing else but worship him!

Surprise Surprise!

I dreamt death came the other night
And heaven's gate swung wide;
With kindly grace an angel came
To usher me inside.

Yet there to my astonishment
Stood folks I'd known on earth,
Some I had judged as quite unfit
Or of but little worth.

Indignant words rose to my lips
But never were set free;
For every face showed stunned surprise
NO ONE expected me!

(Anonymous)

Chapter 15
LOVE

"We seem to have covered quite a lot, don't we! I have a lot to think about."

"Remember, don't just think about it, speak to God about it."

"Yes I will but if you had to sum it all up in one or two words then I don't suppose you would find that very easy."

"Yes I would and actually I would only really need one word."

"Oh? What's that then?"

"The word is love. The Bible tells us that God is love and this really sums up everything. 'For God so loved the world that he gave his one and only Son, that whoever believes in him shall not perish but have eternal life (John 3:16).' All that he has done has been done because of love. We will never be able to understand why God loves us as he does but there can be no doubt about it.

"I hadn't realized before how much he has done. When you went through it all in the first part of the book it does seem a lot. God created the world and humankind to live here during time (and I suppose he also created time!); then Jesus came to earth as a baby and lived here to show us what God is like. Then, most marvellous of all, Jesus died on the cross to demonstrate God's love to us. I must say that does affect me."

"I am so glad to hear it because it never stops affecting me when I think about such love."

"Then Jesus rose again and is today alive in heaven which means I can have a relationship with him."

"Yes that's great – you have actually read all this – thank you!"

"But there's more. God is willing to give us the gift of the Holy Spirit so that we are able to know him – that sounds wonderful too."

"Yes it certainly is – we can do nothing to please God without the Holy Spirit."

"And we also cannot please God without faith – I remember that bit – and we have the Bible which is the Word of God to teach us all about him. I really must get into that a bit because some of it does sound quite interesting."

"Oh I really hope you do read it because I am sure that if you really do commit to doing so you will find it a wonderful book."

"Oh and also I remember the final bit in part one was about God revealing himself in the Father, the Son and the Holy Spirit. He really has done so much for us – I never realized that before."

"So surely you can see why this is all summed up in one word – love."

"Yes I think I can."

"And the more I appreciate that love the more I will want to respond to it in the way I live my life. We all want to please those we love so if I love God then obviously I will want to please him. In fact, if what I do is not because of love then it won't be worth much because love is the most important thing of all. 'Love therefore is the whole law (Romans 13:10); 'for he that loves another has fulfilled the law (Romans 13:8).' That says it all really doesn't it.

"Yes I suppose it does. That makes it all quite simple doesn't it – I wonder why I have made it so complicated?"

"We do tend to complicate things unnecessarily. If we just took God at his word then life would be a lot simpler! But you know, there is something you have to do to get any benefit from all this."

"What's that?"

"You have to believe it! The Bible says, 'Everyone who calls on the name of the Lord will be saved.' Oh how I hope and pray that you will do that and not just forget about all we have spoken about."

I have to end this final chapter of my book with love! We began by talking about our Creator God who made this beautiful world and allowed humankind to live here in time. The God who loves me (and you) so much that he sent his only Son to die for me (and you). The God to whom we belong twice over – created and redeemed. The God who loves us so much that he wants our company while we are here on earth, in time, and then for all eternity. A God who wants us to know him and to have a relationship with him.

Knowing God's love

So, how do I know I know God? I know with total conviction that I know him because I have a relationship with him. The previous chapter gives a very specific example of God working in my life. There are many more such examples – far too many to include here. Perhaps these will be the subject of another book. For now my passionate desire is for *you* to know personally the love of God. I know his great love for me because Jesus died for me and that great love was demonstrated at the cross. I know his great love for me because he has provided everything that I need to know him and to have a relationship with him. I know his great love constantly in every aspect of my life here on earth as I journey through time to eternity. I know his great love on a daily basis and I long for you to know it too.

He speaks to me and listens to me – because he loves me. He allows me the freedom to be me – because he loves me. The highs and the lows I experience in my life – are because he loves me. The suffering and sorrow that I sometimes experience – are because he loves me. He has made an eternal commitment to me – because he loves me. He challenges me and helps me to understand myself and more about him – because he loves me. He has placed me in his family with others who also know him – because he loves me. His

122

love is true love and his love never fails. Why would you not want to know such love?

God's love will deal with evil

I have heard people say that if God is a God of love then surely there can be no hell. A loving God would not punish evil, so they think. What kind of love would it be if it allowed evil to continue to ruin everything? It is *because* God is love that he will eventually punish evil and it will no longer be allowed to cause sorrow and suffering and death. Evil will one day be put away for ever, together with all those who choose to reject God's love and all that he has provided. It is because God is love that he has not yet done this. He is waiting patiently for many more to come to know him and his love in the intervening time but he will not wait for ever. No one knows when the day will be that God will step into this world again. The Bible tells us that Jesus *will* come again, not to die on a cross, but to reign as a king. In the meantime, why would you not want to know such a wonderful person?

Questions

I have written this book because of all the questions I have been asked by various people and because of all the questions that I have asked myself. We make it more complicated than it needs to be with all our questions but God is so patient and so gracious. He is ready and willing to hear you immediately you call out to him. Oh that his love would penetrate into your heart so that you realize your need of him and invite him into your life. Accept that you have no righteousness of your own, you are a sinner. Accept that Jesus died for *you* and thank him for it. Invite him into your life and you will never regret it for a moment. I can tell you this from my own experience and I am not the only one! Millions of Christians alive today can tell you the same thing and millions more will agree when we all meet together in eternity. What love!

There is so much at stake. Surely you would not want to miss out? We began by asking, 'what if it's true after all' and if you are still not sure then please don't rest until you are sure. How can you refuse such love? Why would you not want such a marvellous relationship with such a wonderful person?

Love never fails

And so, it is only as we begin to know God's love that we can really understand what true love is. I know I know God because I know a little of his love and because of that I am challenged to try to show that love to others. Below is a well-known Scripture which sums up this chapter far better than I ever could and for this reason I quote it in its entirety.

1 Corinthians 13

If I speak in the tongues of men or of angels, but do not have love, I am only a resounding gong or a clanging cymbal. If I have the gift of prophecy and can fathom all mysteries and all knowledge, and if I have a faith that can move mountains, but do not have love, I am nothing. If I give all I possess to the poor and give over my body to hardship that I may boast, but do not have love, I gain nothing.

Love is patient, love is kind. It does not envy, it does not boast, it is not proud. It does not dishonour others, it is not self-seeking, it is not easily angered, it keeps no record of wrongs. Love does not delight in evil but rejoices with the truth. It always protects, always trusts, always hopes, always perseveres.

Love never fails. But where there are prophecies, they will cease; where there are tongues, they will be stilled, where there is knowledge, it will pass away. For we know in part and we prophesy in part, but when completeness comes, what is in part disappears. When I was a child, I talked like a child, I thought like a child, I reasoned like a child. When I became a man, I put the ways of childhood behind me. For now we see only a reflection as in a mirror; then we shall see face to face. Now I know in part; then I shall know fully, even as I am fully known.

And now these three remain: faith, hope and love. But the greatest of these is love.

EPILOGUE

You have come to the end of this book, but you are now at the beginning of the rest of your life. If you already know God then my passionate desire is that you will continue to grow in that knowledge (Colossians 1:10) and deepen your relationship with him. Perhaps though you do not know God and in that case I now speak directly to you and ask you to read this epilogue as though your life depends on it – because your eternal life may well do so.

I am asking you now to forget, for the moment, whether you thought this book was good, bad or indifferent. Whatever your view of this book, you now have a decision to make. You cannot avoid it. Doing nothing is a decision in itself. It is between God and you personally. No one else can make this decision for you, it is for you alone. You can either accept or reject the love of God. You can either accept or reject the wonderful sacrifice Jesus made on your behalf on the cross. You can either invite Jesus into your life or you can close the door. The choice is yours – entirely yours.

One day you will actually meet Jesus face to face. You may have sixty, seventy, eighty or even ninety years here – surely this cannot compare with eternity! But after your death comes the judgement. You can either meet with Jesus as a Saviour – because you have accepted all he has done on your behalf – or as a Judge. I have heard people say that they will leave their decision until they are on their death bed. But some people never get such a chance on their death bed. Even if you do, you will have missed out on some of the greatest experiences here on earth. Many people die in an instant with no time to consider anything. Please don't miss the chance now of accepting Jesus into your life because, who knows, tomorrow it may be too late.

Just You[10]

You are not an accident.
Even at the moment of your conception,
out of many possibilities
only certain cells combined,
survived, grew to be you.
You are unique.
You were created for a purpose.
God loves you.

"For God so loved the world that he gave his one and only Son, that
whoever believes in him shall not perish but have eternal life"
(John 3:16).

BIBLIOGRAPHY

Chapter Two

1. Graham Kendrick – *Songs of Fellowship* (Kingsway Music 1998) song number 390 (meekness and majesty)

Chapter Three

2. Anselm – *Anselm of Canterbury The Major Works* (Oxford University Press Great Clarendon Street Oxford OX2 6DP 1998) p349

3. Anselm – *Anselm of Canterbury The Major Works* (Oxford University Press Great Clarendon Street Oxford OX2 6DP 1998) p320

Chapter Five

4. Anselm – *Anselm of Canterbury The Major Works* (Oxford University Press Great Clarendon Street Oxford OX2 6DP 1998) p87

5. Charles H Spurgeon – *My Conversion* (Springdale USA: Whitaker House, 1996) p93

6. Ethel Romig Fuller - *Radio* - http://www.clarion-call.org/prayer/viewpnt.html

Chapter Six

7. Dave Bilbrough - *Songs of Fellowship* (Kingsway Music 1998) song number 197

Chapter Seven

8. Lee Strobel – *Celtic Daily Prayer* (Collins, a division of HarperCollinsPublishers
77-85 Fulham Palace Road London W6 8JB 2005) p 402

Chapter Eight

9. Ralph Wouldham – *Celtic Daily Prayer* (Collins, a division of HarperCollinsPublishers 77-85 Fulham Palace Road London W6 8JB 2005) p348

Epilogue

10. A prayer of blessing – *Celtic Daily Prayer* (Collins, a division of HarperCollinsPublishers 77-85 Fulham Palace Road London W6 8JB 2005) p300

About the author

Margaret Weston is the author of the BSBP series and the 'How do I know?' series. Margaret would love to hear from you with any comments about her books at info@howdoiknowbooks.co.uk

'How do I know?' Series

The 'How do I know?' series consists of an ongoing conversation between two people. **'How do I know I know God?'** is the first book in the series.

'How do I know what God wants me to do?' is the second book in the series and is written as a challenge to the author herself and to Christians world-wide. Will you realise your potential in Christ? Will you take action - or if you are already doing so, will you continue to take action - to advance God's kingdom in our generation?

The third book in the series is **'How do I know God answers prayer?'** which is a question every Christian should be able to answer! However, the book also looks at the subject of prayer in a wider sense as the two unknown people continue to discuss this subject together. You will find questions that are often asked by those who know God and also those who do not.

BSBP Series

The BSBP (Bible Studies for Busy People) series is intended to be for a specific group of people – those who really want to study the Bible but find they simply do not have the time. Life can be so hectic and whilst there are many very good Bible studies and commentaries available, these can be quite off-putting for very busy people.

The studies do not claim to be an in-depth look at a particular book of the Bible. They are meant to be used as an overview and to help the reader obtain a good grasp of the subject matter without having to use hours of their time.

Full details of all the books in both the **'How do I know?'** and the **BSBP series** can be found on the following websites. The books are all available from Amazon and selected bookstores.

http://www.howdoiknowbooks.com

https://www.amazon.com/author/margaretweston

30869744R00076

Made in the USA
Charleston, SC
29 June 2014